Organic
Pest Control

for Home & Garden

by Tom Roberts

Book Publishing Company

The author wishes to thank the many people involved in the production of this book. Some contributed directly and others indirectly. To each of them our heartfelt thanks.

We would also like to thank a certain lovely dragonfly that kept us company one day on the steps of our house next to the garden while writing parts of this book. Every now and then she would take off and do a loopty-loop in the air with her noisy wings and land right back beside us for a while then fly off again to catch another mosquito or leafhopper. We finally had to abandon our sunny steps because we kept putting down our pens and pencils and watching intently the marvels of our garden and our world.

Author's Note: Special thanks to the following people—Dorothy Bates, W.O. Wilson, Eleanor Dale Evans, Bob and Cynthia Holzapfel, and Richard Martin.

Formerly *Shepherd's Purse*
Design and Layout: Eleanor Dale Evans; Illustrations: Richard Martin
Revised Edition Copyright © 1998 Tom Roberts

Published by Book Publishing Company, PO Box 99,
Summertown, TN 38483 (888) 260-8458

14 13 12 11 10 09 08   10 9 8 7 6 5

ISBN10 1-57067-052-8   **ISBN13 978-57067-052-7**

Roberts, Tom (Tom D.)
    Organic pest control for home & garden / by Tom Roberts, --Rev. ed.
        p.   cm.
    Rev. ed. of: Shepherd's Purse / by Pest Publications. c1987
    Includes bibliographical references (p.   ) and index.
    ISBN 1-57067-052-8
    1. Insect pests--Biological control--Handbooks, manuals, etc.
2. Insect pests--Control--Handbooks, manuals, etc. 3. Organic gardening. I. Shepherd's purse. II. Title.
SB933.3.R635 1997
635'.0497--dc21   97-48311
                                            CIP

Every effort has been made to present safe controls, but the use of them is at the reader's risk. Reference to commercial products and their trade names is made for purposes of clarity and no discrimination of other companies with similar products is implied.

Book Publishing Co. is a member of Green Press Initiative. We chose to print this title on paper with postconsumer recycled content, processed without chlorine, which saved the following natural resources:

919 pounds of solid waste	7,153 gallons of water
1,723 pounds of greenhouse gases	20 trees
14 million BTU of energy	

For more information, visit <www.greenpressinitiative.org>. Savings calculations thanks to the Environmental Defense Paper Calculator, <www.papercalculator.org>.

CONTENTS

APPENDIX

Introduction

Most gardeners encounter an insect problem during the growing season. Insects, good and bad, are the most common "wild animals" we observe in the garden. The question most gardeners ask is "What do I do about the bugs?" There is no absolute answer to that question, but we plan to outline some alternatives to the use of persistent or broad range poisons. This outline should help you with your own experimentation, the trial and error process that is a large part of the fun and delight in gardening.

Some preventive measures, cultural and biological, are necessary for insect management. We have found that doing nothing or very little else in the way of insect control turns out to be the safest and most effective insect management. Every now and then pest populations can get out of balance and we have to do something about the bugs, but that happens far less than we ever could have imagined when we first began gardening.

Most beginning gardeners anticipate every plant will be eaten down to the ground if something is not done about the bugs. After the first season we realized how foolish our anxieties really were and it was only our lack of experience and knowledge that contributed to that fear.

Biological Control

For gardening purposes the word "control" means maintaining pest populations within a tolerable range. What you want to tolerate is up to you. Usually control does not mean elimination or eradication. Eradication can be impossible, expensive and dangerous.

Biological control simply implies using living organisms or their products to control pests. It has successfully controlled pest plants (weeds), pest insects and even pest rabbits (vertebrates).

Biological techniques may involve simple things such as:

1. Handpicking
2. Use of natural predators (organisms that eat pests whole)
3. Parasites (organisms that eat pests from the inside)
4. Microbials (microscopic organisms that make pests sick)
5. Companion planting, where one plant protects another
6. Natural scents (pheromones) and tastes to repel, trap or confuse insects

Organic Insect Control

Organic control involves all the biological control methods listed above with three additional considerations:

1. Soil health and fertility (composting, etc.)
2. Knowledge of insect biology to allow for cultural controls like crop rotation
3. Trapping—using simple physical controls

Integrated Pest Management

Integrated pest management, or IPM, is similar to the concepts above and is useful for both commercial situations and home, yard, and garden settings. On occasion IPM uses synthetic pest poisons, if necessary. Some IPM concepts useful for gardeners to keep in mind are:

1. Identify pest insects, understand their biology and natural enemies.
2. Monitor insect population densities either directly or with traps.
3. Determine level of plant injury related to population densities.
4. If population is above a threshold of tolerance, use a combination of control strategies including natural enemies (biological control), cultural controls and selective pesticides.
5. Evaluate the effect of the strategy by monitoring. (Back to step 2)

IPM aims to work with natural balances as much as possible. Commercial farmers like its cost effectiveness and how it often avoids insect resistance and environmental problems. Monitoring is the heart of IPM.

A Word About Plant Diseases

Many plant diseases are spread by insects or caused by soil fertility imbalance. House plants that become diseased are usually attacked by whitefly and aphids. These inconspicuous insects suck plant juices by piercing plant tissues. They transmit viruses that they inject into plants with their saliva. Further, the wounds they make start to decay and are susceptible to airborne diseases that land on the wounds. Spraying the plants with soap or releasing *Encarsia Formosa* (whitefly parasite) in the house will prevent plant injury.

Aphids also excrete a sweet juice called honeydew. Honeydew can become a breeding place for molds. Sometimes removing the honeydew with a cotton swab will prevent diseases like sooty mold. However, the root cure for many diseases is removing the insect spreading the disease.

Diseased outdoor plants may indicate that soil fertility has declined beyond the point of supporting the plants. However, even with good fertility, old plants become susceptible to disease. Citrus orchards are replanted after a number of years for this reason. The best remedy is to replant with young plants.

The gardener can spread disease in the garden by handling wet plants or by touching a diseased leaf and then handling other plants. Cut off and destroy diseased leaves and wash your hands before touching another plant. Some disease organisms live in the soil. Compost heats up considerably as it forms and is free of most soil borne diseases.

Insect control and good soil enriched by compost are the keys to avoiding most disease problems. Crop rotation also prevents plant diseases in the garden.

Biological Insect Control

Augmenting Beneficial Organisms

Unknown to most beginning gardeners, there are many beneficial parasites and predators that are natural enemies of pests. Sometimes natural controls are already present in your garden, but are either in very small numbers or their build-up is delayed. Here the gardener does well to augment the beneficial organisms. Increasing their number may involve early or concentrated release of them.

Beneficial insects, either naturally occurring or commercially bought, often require nectar, pollen and water. Blooming flowers provide nectar and pollen. We suggest that your garden contain flowers that are varied enough in type to be in bloom as much of the year as possible. For a water source to increase the humidity in the garden, we recommend digging two or three holes about 10 inches in diameter and 8 inches deep, fit with clay flower pots and fill with water. If mosquitoes are a problem, one small briquet of Bti (page 10) or Bti spray in each hole or flower pot will control mosquitoes. Successive wetting and drying will not affect the potency of Bti, but it will dissolve over time and need to be replaced.

Toads eat many insects. You can encourage them to work in your garden by placing an inverted clay flower pot with a large hole chipped out of the rim placed in the shade near a water hole to provide a nice home.

Braconids are another example of nature helping the gardener. They are small wasps that sting large pest caterpillars like tomato hornworms. As they sting, they lay eggs into the caterpillar. The eggs hatch and braconid larvae develop in the living caterpillar. Finally the larvae eat through the caterpillar's skin, usually on its back. Here they immediately spin cocoons that resemble small rice grains, The caterpillar is still alive, but it will soon die, leaving the adult wasps to hatch and attack other caterpillars. We don't have to buy this naturally occurring insect.

Unfortunately these little fellows and other helpful organisms are often more sensitive than the pests to pesticides, or broad spectrum poisons. These poisons kill a wide range of insects and living things. Since there are fewer numbers of beneficial parasites and predators, poisons destroy the delicate balance of nature between helpful and harmful insects. Carbaryl (Sevin) and malathion are examples of broad spectrum petroleum based poisons often recommended by some county agents and dispensed by discount stores.

We also caution against the indiscriminate use of broad spectrum botanical poisons like rotenone and pyrethrin with piperonyl butoxide. These botanical poisons can kill most any insect including beneficial ones. They do break down quickly though, and don't persist in the environment like some synthetic poisons. Still, care should be exercised. We recommend them for occasional spot treatments of acute problems, but not for spraying every plant. Rotenone is a poison.

Commercially Available Organisms

Commercially available beneficial insects are listed for each pest insect in this book. The following is a discussion of three beneficial insects that should be used for general control of many insects in the yard and garden. For home gardens we suggest using the smallest amount available, applying three releases at two week intervals in the early spring when flowers are blooming after the last frost. An early fall release may be necessary in areas with a long growing season.

Trichogramma are insects no bigger than the period at the end of this sentence. They sting pest eggs and lay their own eggs inside them. Trichogrammid larvae hatch and kill the pest eggs. They are sold commercially on cards of about 400 parasitized eggs. When they arrive, the trichogramma adults are just about to emerge from the eggs and begin their life cycle. These minute beneficial insects help protect Texas cotton and Washington apples from different caterpillar pests.

A trichogramma release stand can be made in gardens from a one foot stake driven a few inches into the ground. Halfway up the stake apply a two inch band of petroleum jelly all around to keep ants away from the eggs. Staple or tack the card with trichogramma to the side of the stake near the top. Then as a final measure to protect the card from rain, staple or tack a three inch cardboard "roof" to the top of the stake. Most trichogramma hatch and fly away within three days, but leave the card undisturbed for a week to allow for cooler weather or slowpokes. Lightly water the garden for about two weeks after the release to ensure the first generation's survival. Hot dry weather causes the greatest loss of trichogramma. Warm humid weather with rain provides ideal conditions for their growth and production of succeeding generations.

During winters, trichogramma populations decrease drastically, so you need to release them every spring. Their chances of survival over winter is uncertain and even if they do survive, there may not be enough of them to help you unless you supply more.

Lacewings are net-winged, pale green insects that flutter like butterflies. They are available from several companies; check the list of suppliers in the appendix. Their alligator-shaped larvae are voracious predators of pest insects.

Ladybug (ladybird) beetles and their larvae are also valuable predators of aphids and other pests and pest eggs. To encourage them to remain in the garden you can provide some food for them, called "wheast". You can buy wheast when you buy ladybugs or ask for a recipe. Delaying application of ladybugs until garden plants are larger and flowers are blooming is an alternative to providing wheast for them.

Praying mantis egg masses can be bought and set in your garden. They hatch into minute insects that grow to be effective, beneficial predators. During walks in the woods in the fall you may spot egg masses that you can clip off for free. Clip off the whole mass on its twig. Don't bring them inside or the heat may kill them or hatch them too soon. Place them in a protected bush outside for the winter near you garden. Goldenrod is a favored habitat of the praying mantis.

Control with Micro-Organisms (Microbials)

Insects have their own diseases much like plants do. The insect disease organisms are naturally present in your garden already, but at too low a level to balance pest populations. To achieve a balance, increase them. This is microbial control. Several microbial control agents are commercially available to help you. They are very selective and are harmless to good insects. This is important, since you don't want to disturb good insects the way broad spectrum poisons do. The following table lists some available microbial controls. (Mention of *Ringer* products is for illustration only. Many other manufacturers produce similar products.)

Commercially Available Microbial Controls

Microbial Control	Product	Pest	Characteristics
Bacillus thuringiensis (Bt)	Ringer Vegetable Insect Attack or Ringer Caterpillar Attack	only caterpillars	sprayed or dusted, must be eaten by the insect
Bacillus thuringiensis israelensis (Bti) special strain of Bt	Ringer Mosquito Attack	only mosquito and blackfly larvae	kills larvae in water, sprayed or applied as a floating ring
Bacillus popilliae (milky spore disease)	Ringer Grub Attack	grubs of Japanese beetles	applied to soil, very long lasting
Insect-eating nematodes (Nc)	Scanmask, others	soil pests, boring pests	seeks out pests, several ways to apply
Nosema locustae	Ringer Grasshopper Attack	grasshoppers and some types of crickets	applied as bait, must be eaten by the insect
Codling Moth Granulosis virus (CMGV)	Decyd ™	caterpillars of codling moth	must be eaten by the insect
Nuclear polyhedrosis virus (NPV)	Gypchek ™	gypsy moth caterpillars	must be eaten by the insect
Bt (sd) BT San Diego	Ringer Colorado Potato Beetle Attack	Colorado potato beetle, elmleaf beetle	must be eaten by the insect

Bt cell with
spore and crystal

Mature cell
ruptures

Bacillus Thuringiensis or "Bt" is a rod shaped bacterium. Bt is sold as a mixture of the resting spore stage and diamond-shaped protein crystals that form near the spores. It affects only caterpillars that eat it. The crystals stop the insects' feeding, then the spores germinate and the insects die. Packages of Bt can be stable for as many as ten to fifteen years, but is inactivated by direct sunlight after a couple of weeks. It is sold as *Thuricide, Dipel, Caterpillar Attack, Ringer Vegetable Insect Attack* and others.

Bti (*Bacillus thuringiensis israelensis*) is a special strain of Bt active only against mosquito wrigglers and blackfly larvae in water. It too must be eaten to kill them. It is safe for all beneficial aquatic insects like mayflies. One can either spray Bti or toss floating rings of it onto water. It is sold as *Mosquito Attack, Vectobac,* etc.

Bacillus Popilliae is a soil inhabiting bacterium. It infects only grubs of the Japanese beetle and a few species of June beetles. It turns the normally clear blood of these grubs a milky color, so it's also known as "milky spore disease". All the grubs feed on roots and are pests. However, it does not kill several species of pest grubs, so precise grub identification by your county agent or lawn and garden center is necessary to be sure you have a grub it will work on. Since Japanese beetle grubs are the most common ones, some people just treat with milky spore as a preventative.

Milky spore is sold under trade names *Doom* and *Ringer Grub Attack.* Apply it to grassy areas and around orchards where adult beetles lay eggs and grubs develop. After application, allow one to two years for it to spread through the soil. One application of milky spore can last up to 20 years. Both grubs and adults damage plants so control the beetles by controlling the grubs.

Insect-eating nematodes (Nc; *Neoaplectana carpocapsae,* alternately named *Steinernematoda carpocapsae*) are beneficial, microscopic, thread-like relatives of the worm family which attack and parasitize many pest insects. They were first discovered in America in codling moth larvae in Beltsville, Maryland, but since then have been found in almost every geographical area in low concentrations. Over 230 different pests are susceptible to them, including squash vine borers and cucumber beetles. Nc nematodes actively seek out the insects they prey upon. They will crawl into borer holes if they are sprayed or injected very close to their burrows.

Just as there are good and bad insects with different life styles, so there are different kinds of nematodes. Most nematodes are free-living and are present in all soil where they help to break down solid organic material, such as in compost. A few other nematodes attack some plant roots. Nc nematodes are different; they only attack pest insects and feed on them where there is a moist, dark environment such as in soil.

Nematodes enter the insect they attack either through its mouth or the spiracles, the breathing tube passages. They enter the blood-filled body cavity and begin feeding. Their method of entry into the cavity is by sheer mechanical force, not a chemical reaction. While feeding, they release a bacterium in their intestines which is emitted in the fecal material they expel. The bacterium "mummifies" the insect or preserves it

11

while the nematodes feed and reproduce inside. The insect usually dies within 24 hours after the nematodes have entered its mouth. Ten to fourteen days later nematodes emerge through the host insect's body wall and search for new insects to infect. During this stage their digestive system has collapsed and they do not feed. Their entire body is enclosed in a sheath of cells called a cuticle. They shed this cuticle after they enter the host insect's digestive midgut and before they force their way between the cells of the host insect's intestinal wall. Some nematodes can live in soil for 12 to 15 months without feeding.

Nc nematodes are shipped in a topsoil or peatmoss-like medium for application on the soil. Other producers ship them on a moist sponge. Trade names are *Grub-eater* and *Scanmask* as well as others.

These beneficial nematodes can dry out and die, but a soil that supports plant growth is moist enough for nematodes to survive. When first putting them out though, be careful to have a moist soil and avoid sunlight. Apply at dusk to presoaked soil or wet tree trunks. This helps the nematodes move around.

Nosema locustae is a one-celled protozoan parasite that is mixed into a cereal bait (wheat bran) that kills grasshoppers and crickets. The resting spore stage is sold as *Nolo* and *Grasshopper Attack*. Maximum effect is achieved a year after application.

Codling Moth Granulosis Virus (CMGV) and Nuclear-Polyhedrosis Virus (NPV) are two viruses that affect some pest insects and not others. They are rather potent, but must be eaten to be effective. Similar virus diseases of other pests also exist, explaining why grinding up dead or sick insects and spraying the suspension may help kill other pests. There is a different strain of NPV for each different insect.

Viruses are obligate parasites of living cells. All known biological life can be classified into six major kingdoms.
1. Bacteria
2. Viruses
3. Protozoa
4. Fungi
5. Plant
6. Animal

Companion Planting

Companion planting or repellent planting means mixing plants in a row so that plants with odors, tastes or other characteristics repellent to pests are planted next to host plants that they like and damage. The insects find the mix of plants not to their liking and leave the garden for a better place to feed. An example is interplanting radishes with cucumbers to repel cucumber beetles. Another is larkspur to repel Japanese beetles. Finding which plants work best for this interplanting is a matter of trial and error in each geographical location.

Mixing flowers in a vegetable garden will help, but may attract some unwanted pests. Further, some plants inhibit others. The following table is a list of further suggestions with which to begin your own experimentation.

Suggested Companion Plantings

Pest	Plant Repellent
Ants	spearmint, tansy, pennyroyal
Bean Leaf Beetle	potato, onion, turnip
Codling Moth	common oleander
Colorado Potato Beetle	green beans, coriander, nasturtium
Cowpea Curculio	garlic, cloves, radish
Cucumber Beetle	radish, tansy
Flea Beetle	garlic, onion, mint
Harlequin Bug	radish, turnips, onion
Imported Cabbage Worm	mint, sage, rosemary, hyssop
Japanese Beetle	garlic, larkspur, red buckeye
Leafhopper	geranium
Mexican Bean Beetle	potato, onion, garlic, radish
Root-Knot Nematodes	French marigold
Spider Mites	onion, garlic, cloves
Squash Bug	radish, marigold
Squash Vine Borer	cloves, onion, garlic
Stink Bug	radishes
Tarnished Plant Bug	garlic, pepper
Thrips	marigold
Tomato Hornworm	marigold, sage
Whitefly	marigold, nasturtium

Traps

Closely related to the ideas of companion planting is the use of products that confuse, lure or trap pests. However, all insect traps are not a good choice even if they are effective. Black light traps kill many valuable beneficial insects like lacewings and trichogramma, but few mosquitoes or other pests. We don't recommend them. Light traps can be useful for monitoring purposes and used with a funnel trap to control some adult stage beetles like June beetles.

The commercial traps available use floral or plant scents or specific sexual scents (pheromones) from specific insects to lure pests. A good example is Ringer Beetle Trap Attack for Japanese beetle control. They may also use certain attractive colors, like yellow. Here again, use caution as some of these commercial traps may be too powerful. If you hang up a trap for Japanese beetles, place it away from sensitive plants, like rose bushes, so the beetles will be lured away from there.

You can also make your own trap with "tanglefoot" resins. It can be applied around some trees and bushes to prevent ants and other flightless pests from climbing. Smearing "tanglefoot" on a red plastic apple hung in apple trees will catch the flies that breed apple maggots. (See Glossary for definition of terms.)

Cultural Insect Control

Crop rotation helps enrich soil and control insect. It means changing the type of plant at a particular garden location from one year to the next. Generally, three years between planting of vegetables in the same family or class is best. Small gardens may have to be moved after several years in order to achieve good crop rotation.

Good garden sanitation is also important. If you remove diseased or rotting fruit, you will help remove insect hiding places and food.

Another important insect control is fall plowing. Most beginning gardeners forget this task and by doing so create insect problems the following spring. If you plow all old plants and vines under in the fall, many eggs and insects are crushed or dried out. Others are exposed for birds to eat. Some gardeners combine planting a cover crop with fall plowing. After plowing, sprinkle some clover or rye seeds over the soil, rake them in lightly and water. Be sure to use enough seeds to give a thick stand, ¼ to ½ pound of clover seeds/1000 square feet. Plow the clover under the following spring.

Alternate planting methods can also contribute to cultural control. Most people plant their gardens in traditional single rows. An alternative is beds or wide rows. For instance, beds can be two feet wide with a pathway or walkway along the side. There's no need for boards or lumber in making flat beds such as these. This method prevents soil compaction and provides insect control. If vegetables and/or flowers are planted randomly and alternately in beds instead of single file, some insects will be confused, have trouble finding a plant to eat and leave the garden.

Row covers made of cheese cloth netting purchased from a grocery store or cotton based netting closely woven and commercially available, will help deter pests such as Japanese beetles and leafminers.

Acute Insect Control

A Word for Safety

The word "safe" can be applied to drinking water. All other garden chemicals, homemade and commercial, are questionable. This is especially true of cycloheximide and other seed and leaf fungicides. Consult your medical doctor or poison control center if in doubt. Compressed air sprayers and dust should not be used without a protective mask available at hardware stores. Diatomaceous earth may cause lung silicosis if inhaled and kills some beneficial insects, as well. Always read the label and use eye protection.

Sprays

Insecticidal soaps are special soap solutions to be sprayed on insects. They create a thin film that blocks the tubes that all insects breathe through. These fine branching tubes can be blocked by even the thinnest of soap films. However, soap residues on leaf surfaces have no effect on insects or other animals, so the soap spray must be sprayed directly on the insects. Be sure to spray the underside of leaves where many insects are found. When it is recommended for use on caterpillars, it is most effective on smaller ones. Commercial insecticidal soaps are mild and do not burn plants. Some are formulated for flowers, others for vegetables and fruit, dependent on the carriers used. Some commercial insect soaps have as much as 30% alcohol content, even though their label does not state this. Soap spray can adversely affect many beneficials, including dragonflies, so you might use it as spot spraying only.

Homemade soap sprays can also kill insects, interacting chemically with the outer membrane of the insect. Since they can also burn plant leaves, trial and error should be used to determine the brand of soap and concentration you use. We recommend starting with 2-3 tablespoons per gallon of water. Rinse off the plants with water after an hour or two if you are not willing to experiment. This should be sufficient time to affect the insects, but not harm the plants. Soaps with perfume and dyes are not recommended. We've found some liquid dishwashing soaps so mild they can be left on the plants.

Ordinary agricultural lime, used at ¼ to ½ cup per gallon of water, makes another homemade spray that kills some insects and mites and dries out many smaller insects. Its effectiveness depends upon the insect's surface area and weight. Spider mites are tiny "bugs" that are affected by lime. Generally, most insect larvae are sensitive as are others like aphids. Soap and lime mixed together make a potent double-acting spray with the soap helping the lime stick to the insect. Lime also acts as an irritant for adult insects even if it does not kill them. When using lime dust on wet plants, you might want to rinse it off with water after one or two days. Some plants might have an adverse reaction to either soap or lime. Do a trial spraying on a few leaves and wait two or three days to determine the plant's reaction before spraying the whole plant. Vegetables such as cabbage and broccoli like lime. Again, it's a matter of experimentation. We spot spray lime in the garden like we spot spray with soap. Caution: do not overuse lime, because it may change soil PH levels. Compost acts as a good chemical buffer, though, to counteract either too acid or too alkaline soil conditions.

Homemade repellents can be made of garlic, onion, or pepper juices. Insects are not poisoned, but plant surfaces are made repellent either to taste or touch. One recipe uses a garlic clove, one small onion, and ¼ teaspoon cayenne pepper added to one quart water plus one teaspoon liquid dishwashing detergent to make the spray stick to leaves. We found that substituting several hot pepper pods for the cayenne pepper makes a more effective mixture. Finely chop the vegetables or juice them in a blender, then strain the juice through cheese cloth. When working with hot peppers, be careful to protect your hands from the burning juice with rubber gloves.

Handpicking

Handpicking is the oldest known form of insect control. Insects are picked from plants and crushed. Insects like adult potato beetles and tomato horn worms are easily controlled by handpicking. Wear gloves to avoid allergic reactions. Handpicking is actually a biological control, but since it is so fast, we include it under acute controls.

To make the job easier, hose off plants to discourage aphids, spider mites and some other insects who dislike being wet. For another trick, use a small glass jar with ¼ inch of water in the bottom. Hold the jar slightly under a leaf, then flick the bug into the water.

A butterfly net can be made of two coat hangers and a two yard piece of cheese cloth. Capturing one moth in the spring means two to three hundred less cabbage worms to eat your broccoli.

If enough insects are handpicked in spring and early summer, succeeding generations may be severely reduced.

Microbials

Bt and beneficial Nc nematodes are also fast acting biologicals for certain insects and can be considered acute controls.

Creating a Good Garden Environment

We believe that insects attack weak, diseased plants and act as "nature's pruners." A rich soil grows healthy plants which resist insect attack. Each plant requires a unique soil for optimum growth; some require more nitrogen than others. Knowing your plants' nutritional requirements will help you control insects more effectively.

Organic Soil Enrichment

We suggest that your soil be enriched over a period of years using among others:

1. Natural microbial fertilizers, such as *Ringer Restore*.
2. Homemade compost, to eventually achieve a 1 foot depth.
3. Composted cow manure.
4. Cottonseed or soybean meal for nitrogen sources.
5. Steamed bone meal or ground rock phosphate for phosphorus sources.
6. Granite dust (about ¼ cup per square foot) or green sand, interacting with a high organic matter content in the soil to create a potassium source.
7. Green manure and mulches.

Most people realize soil in the woods or forest is very rich in humus and good for plants to grow in. There's definitely value in knowing how to make that same woodsy, humus-rich soil in the garden.

Soil contains living micro-organisms, bacteria, fungi, etc., in addition to nonliving particles and humus, decaying organic matter. Chemical fertilizers kill soil micro-organisms, both good and bad, and contribute to nitrate contamination of surface water and water wells. We used commercial fertilizers only when we started gardening, until the soil was enriched with compost, then we discontinued them. A healthy soil is developed over a number of years; it is not an instant process.

Compost is easy for homeowners to make. One recipe calls for equal parts, by weight, of fresh grass clippings, fresh fallen leaves and composted cow manure. Shred the leaves by running over them several times with the lawn mower. In the spring and summer when leaves are not available, substitute hay or wheat straw for leaves (if straw mites irritate your skin after working with straw, apply alcohol on your hands, arms and legs, followed by a warm soapy bath). Experienced compost makers can delete the composted cow manure. Make sure the leaves and grass clippings have not been sprayed with pesticides. Mix in clippings and manure, then moisten and pile in a hill. Fasten plastic garbage bags on the top ⅓ of the hill with stones or bricks to contain odor and prevent the pile from drying too quickly. The hill should be neither too moist nor dry.

Depending upon temperature and weather, compost should be ready after four to six weeks in summer or two to four months in winter. Turn the hill once or twice during that time to mix the outside with the inside. The more you turn the hill the faster the compost is made.

If for some reason the composting and decaying process does not take place, add more composted cow manure or cottonseed or soybean meal. To speed things up, make a volcano-like depression in the center to help get air and moisture to the middle of the hill. A compost inoculent like Ringer Compost Maker can increase composting activity and speed. It contains natural soil micro-organisms and sources to increase biological activity.

You can also make compost in plastic garbage bags. Place the ingredients inside a bag and close it with a twist tie. Be sure to perforate the bag with as many small air holes as possible. Turn or shake vigorously 3 or 4 times or more per week to speed up the composting process.

Green manure or cover crops means planting clover, vetch or rye grain seed, then plowing the plants under in the spring.

Weed Control

Weeds are a common gardening problem. Weed seeds may remain viable in the soil for many years. Some can germinate after 25 years. However, seeds buried 2 inches below the surface will not germinate. Some gardeners bury indigenous weed seeds so deeply with compost that they never sprout. Instead of plowing, pull the dying plants up and compost them.

For warmer climates we suggest the following procedure to reduce weed populations. Plow in the early spring. Wait until the weeds start sprouting, then lightly cultivate no more than one inch with a hoe or rake, or spray apple cider vinegar on them. Wait a week or two, then cultivate or spray again. Be careful never to cultivate below an inch or new weed seeds will be brought to the surface, sprout, and grow. Wait another week or two, cultivate or spray, then plant your garden. Of course, watering the garden will force the weeds to germinate faster. Soapy water can be substituted for vinegar to kill very young weed seedlings. Use five tablespoons of liquid dish washing soap per gallon of water. There are differences in soaps, *Ivory* being one that is especially effective, so try several if one doesn't work. The soap or vinegar kills weed leaves which starves the roots. Repeated leaf destruction will eventually destroy the roots entirely.

After your garden comes up, roto-tilling deeply between rows only brings up new weed seeds to the surface. A hand held wick-type applicator filled with soapy water or vinegar can be used between plants and rows after the plants have emerged. Sager Insecticide Soap Company now manufactures a soap based herbicide.

Fight Weeds with Grass Seeds

After a good soaking spring rain walk over the lawn and look for any weeds particularly the broad-leaf weeds and pull them up by the roots. Bend over at the waist and at the same time bend your knees a little. Place one arm for support just above the knee on one leg. With the other arm straight down place the thumb and finger around the stem of the weed. Feel your way down the stem of the weed to the ground. Pull the weed out of the ground root and all. Once you pull one weed out of the ground like this you will not be able to stop yourself from pulling others. Do not therefore do this weed pulling for more than two or three minutes per day. Walk over the lawn looking straight down. The broad-leaf weeds are easy to spot against the thinner narrower blades of grass. Some weeds are harder to control this way as they have the appearance similar to grass. Some of those can be ignored or dealt with differently. Most weeds fall into two categories, either they are winter weeds or summer weeds. Winter weeds grow in the late winter and die back in late spring and early summer. They turn brown and die. Summer weeds emerge in the late spring and grow vigorously in the summer and die in late fall or winter. Plant grass seeds by dropping them from your hand where these weeds have grown after you have pulled them up. Usually there is no need to work the soil with a hoe or rake. Just drop the grass seeds right there and keep that spot well watered. Other weeds may have to be trimmed with a string grass trimmer down to the soil and then grass seeds dropped there. If the weeds seem to be getting ahead of you then spot spray with the vinegar or soap based herbicide or use grass trimmer. Hand pulling the weeds lets you become familiar with the plant; its structure and growth behavior as well as familiarity with your lawn. Simple observation of a problem before it gets too big is the easiest and cheapest way of dealing with a weed problem. Remove any weed seeds that come with the grass seeds you buy as this is the way weeds are being introduced back into the lawn. Use several size wire mesh screens to get the weeds out of the grass seeds available at hardware stores or mail order suppliers. Many seeds come with a fungicide on the seeds be careful and wear gloves and wash off clothes and hands with soap and water. Wear a paper dust mask. Newer seed fungicides could be made from antagonistic fungi but have not been produced even though they have been known for 40 years. Of course you do not have to wait for it to rain in order to pull weeds in the lawn.

A light, weak, acid will kill the plant fungus that grows on the blades and stems of plants including lawn grass. Citric acid made from the oil found in the rind of any citrus fruit can be homemade or the juices of citrus can be sprayed if it is weakened with water, so as not to burn plant leaves. Soaps can be sprayed on the lawn to prevent the spread of fungus, but do not kill the active fungus unless the commercial soap based fungicide is used (Safer soap fungicide and miticide product.) Other homemade products are garlic juice and sulfur as well as the famous Bourdauex mixture, which is lime and copper sulfate. Wear protective equipment when using this product. This product is recommended for fruit trees but not for lawns.

IPM PRINCIPLES

I. THE OBSERVATION
        a. Carnivores verses Herbivores
        b. Natural Antagonists
                1. Their Role
                2. Their Conservation
II. TWO MAJOR LESSONS
        a. Broad Spectrum Verses Target Specific
        b. Injudicious Use
                1. Increase Human Exposure
                2. Insect resistance and controls failure
III. The Answer: ABCs of Insect Management
        a. Biological Control
        b. Cultural Control
        c. Acute Control

The greatest use of knowledge is in knowing when to do nothing or that nothing need be done. Knowledge is the key to understanding and understanding leads to appreciation of things one knows nothing about. In this book we are going to bring you some of that knowledge that you may not have heard about when it comes to insect management in the home or garden or lawn. Hopefully that knowledge will be of use to you as you attempt to find out what to do about the particular insect that is causing a problem for you. Of course there is no absolute answer to that question because the biological world is a complex system. We plan to provide enough information for you to make a knowledgeable decision. Having enough knowledge is the most successful way to manage insect problems. Without knowledge no product used will be as successful as it could or should be. Lack of knowledge combined with lack of experience are the two major reasons why insects are causing a problem.

First let us make two very simple observations about insects in the wild, in their natural habitat in the forest or where ever insects are found. Two major groups occur: those that eat plants and those insects that feed on and eat other insects. "There is no doubt that the greatest single factor in keeping plant-feeding insects from overwhelming the rest of the world is that they are fed upon by other insects."(1) Think about that last sentence for awhile. How long has it been since anyone ever said that to you? Furthermore does not it seem reasonable and likely to be true? We will keep this simple observation in mind when we attempt to give the recommendations of how to control ANY insect.

Second, what other observation can we make that might be important in insect management? Well, it may not be so obvious but implied in the first statement is the fact that the absence of insects that feed on other insects is the major cause of the planet feeding insects being in abundance in a particular situation, be it in the yard or in the home or even in a commercial growing field or greenhouse. These two simple observations; insect-eating insects and anything that destroys them causes the problem are the most important pieces of information that need to be remembered all the time. Therefore a product of pest control that destroys all the insects is the wrong product because it destroys the insect-feeding insects. We call these insects beneficial insects or carnivorous insects. We call the plant-feeding insects that eat plant leaves herbivores. One other important observation to make: if we destroy all the herbivores then the beneficial insects die due to starvation because they have nothing to eat. This situation is to be avoided in pest management because it leads to an outbreak of the herbivores with nothing to keep their population in check.

Now that we know that the plant eating insects have their own naturally occurring antagonists, their own enemies so to speak, are there any other things in the natural environment that kill plant feeding insects? They have their own diseases. These we call the microbial diseases of insects because they are so small that they can only be seen with a microscope. Some of them are bacteria and some are viruses and some are other microscopic living things. We will name them later in this book. So the two major naturally occurring antagonists to any plant eating insect are their parasitoids and predators along with their diseases. Usually there is more that one insect that will eat the plant feeding insect at one of the stages of their life cycle. Either the egg stage or the larval stage or the pupal stage or the adult stage will be attacked by the parasitoids. There is always more than one disease that will kill the plant feeding insect. Out of all these however are those natural antagonists that will kill only that one insect and no others. These we call target specific biologicals. They are either a disease or a target specific parasitoid. These are the products we should use in managing any one target insect because it leaves all the other insects alone.

One other thing that needs to be noted here and that is the role the natural antagonist play in the drama of life. What function do they have in the ecosystem? Is it not obvious that their major function is to reduce the population density of the target insect? Therefore their conservation by not using products that kill the beneficial insects is very important, otherwise they will not be there to eat the plant feeding insects. The word density here means so many insects per square foot of surface area of leaf or some other measure of area or plant. The lessons to be learned from all that has been said is broad spectrum products are out and target specific products are in. Meaning of course the products to be used for safe and effective management of insects. Injudicious use of even the target specific products can cause controls failure and continued use of broad spectrum products can only increase the problems of insects and their growing resistance to chemical controls. The restraint in the use of any product is very important as we will see in the next section when we take up the problem of insects' resistance. The best way to use these new products is within the total context of an integrated pest management technique of using any product only when needed and as monitoring indicates that need.

References:

(1) *IPM for Home and Garden*, Institute for Environmental Studies, University of Illinois (see additional reading section in the Appendix for address and cost.)

(2) *Common Sense Pest Control* by Olkowski, Daar and Olkowski Tauton Press 1991 ISBN# 0-942391-63-2

INSECT RESISTANCE

The term insect resistance is unfamiliar to most gardeners. The phrase refers to the lack of effectiveness of a once useful product. British researchers recently claimed to have discovered the exact mechanism of how insects acquire resistance to a product. This discovery is not of use, for the moment, in designing new hydro-carbon products to defeat the chemical process. The process is too technical to go into here and may not be the final word on the exact sequence of how insects, with their chemistry and genetics, interact with hydro-carbon structures or, for that matter, their diseases. What is known, and simple to explain, is the overt behavior of humans and insects that leads to the problem referred to by the phrase "insect resistance."

First take a relatively small area, for example 10 square acres. Spray a particular product for a specific insect. Out of all the members of that specific insect in that area, one or two are not killed by the product.They have the underlying genetic resistance to that particular product as randomly occurring genetic diversity in nature. Now, what happens over time as these one or two begin to reproduce and multiply in that specific area? The only insects occupying that area are resistant to that product. This situation renders the product useless for controlling that specific insect by the insects passing that trait of resistance on to their offspring.

Unfortunately the problem does not stop there. As the farmer-grower attempts to use a different product to control that insect, its use tends to select those insects with the highest ability to develop resistance in a shorter time frame to all products than the previous generation. This leads over time to a race of insects called "monster bugs," for which there is no available product that is effective. Some of the major commercial crop insect pest have already achieved this distinction. Every year that goes by more insects join the list. Of course we are talking about farming and commercial growing areas and not the 10 acres surrounding the typical home owner or apartment dweller in the cities and suburbs. The problem is there too. The potential problems of a super race of ants, cockroaches, flies, mosquitoes, and fleas are known. Each one of them is resistant to one or more of the usual over used products sold to the unknowledgeable public in spray cans.

Little known by the general public is the history of DDT sprayed in the Panama Canal Zone. In as little as two years, and probably after the first spraying, the product was useless for mosquito control. Other insects in that tropical area are known to have incorporated DDT or its breakdown products DDD and DDE as a means of chemical defense against their parasitoids and predators. Even today their progeny manufacture the molecular structures in their bodies, acting as little chemical factories. The warning this event signaled has not been heeded and the consequences could prove to be tragic for insect pest management. The warning is not to repeat the mistake of underestimating insect response to hydrocarbon molecular structures or their diseases. In 1997 Monsanto Corporation announced the splicing of the Bt genome into corn. It is only a matter of time before this once useful and safe non-hydrocarbon product will be rendered useless as an insecticide due to insect resistance. Possibly the actions of this company will economically injure the non-hydrocarbon industry of one of its better products. It could prove to be the wrong move in the wrong direction, leading to the problem of no effective materials available for pest management. The only conclusion to be reached by this announcement to splice the Bt gene into a plant gene is to call this action Biotechnological Mismanagement.

When every mouthful of corn flakes contains the Bt cell protein crystal in every cell of every corn plant, the human consumption of protein can only increase in a human diet that already includes too much protein. Synthetic sugar substitutes made from a barrel of crude oil and used in soft-drink products, for example, metabolize into proteins in the blood. When the economic forces dictate the decisions then the wrong decisions in the wrong time frame will be made. The consequences could prove to be the calamity of famine. Biotechnology holds great promise but has its requisite down side problems compounded by human greed. For example, genetically altered products are the ones being produced and mass manufactured because they are patentable and this tends to limit the use and availability of the naturally occurring product. Maybe it is time to draw a halt to genetically altered products manufactured for money making purposes only.

Perhaps the best way to manage a powerful biotechnology in the future would be to abandon the Plant Variety Protection Act of the late 1980's which gave patent protection to all biological entities that are genetically altered. Doing that, would change the products presently being researched and would not provide patent protection to any biological product. This would encourage the use of those naturally occurring biological entities that are the endpoint of 400 million years of biological evolution. Certainly they should be the most preferred products to use and to mass manufacture as they might have a longer time frame for effectiveness. There are instances, however, where that has already failed. Rabbits were at one time controlled by a virus and its over use did create a resistance in a relatively short time. Myxomatosis virus for rabbit control in Great Britain is the specific example. This fact is another argument favoring the side that believes the injudicious use of any product can lead to controls failure and the possibility of famine. Over use of a product leads to insect resistance and violates the principles of integrated pest management.

References:

(1) Forgash A. 1984; History, Evolution and consequences of insecticide resistance. *Pesticide Biochem. Physiology.* 22:73-186

(2) *Common Sense Pest Control Quarterly*, Vol (V) -1 Winter 1989 p. 8-12. (see appendix in back of this book for address).

3) Metcalf and Luckman, *Intro to Insect Pest Management.* Wiley Science Series 1975, 587 pages.

COCKROACH IPM for the Home

1. Caulking around pipes
2. Boric Acid in crevices
3. Kitchen garbage can
4. Mop kitchen floor with Borax
5. Spray Pyrethrin barrier
6. Glue boards for monitoring

Cockroaches originally lived in caves and under rocks for protection from their predators. They principally eat decomposing plant and animal matter. So anywhere human food remains are found there the cockroaches will be. More than that is the shelter houses and homes and basements provide the cockroach against their major predator—the birds. To a cockroach a bird no matter how small appears to be a T-REX dinosaur on two feet. Imagine any of the birds the size of a dinosaur. All of us humans would be seeking shelter under rocks and caves in order not to be eaten by the dinosaur size birds. For this reason cockroaches never cross the front yard in the middle of the day in a group of two hundred or more. They simply would not survive the birds descending on them. "That poor bug in that birds beak," as the cartoon character used to say.

So cockroaches stay well hidden during the day in places they feel safe from the birds and any other large animal that might eat them. If they are seen during the day, it means their food source has dwindled to so low a level that they must seek food during the day. Usually this happens due to the population overwhelming and exhausting the food supply. Other reasons could be a lack of water, combined with lack of food, or a summer dry spell, that leads them to migrate to a water source. Water vapor in the air is detected by their antenna and leads them into the house or apartment. Otherwise they are not seen during the day and only come out at night. Many other insects, such as certain crickets, do the same thing. So when the light is turned on in a room at night the cockroaches scurry for a hiding place as they do during the day. They hide in crevices where the birds can not reach them, or in walls where no light and no large animals can disturb them. The baseboards where the floor meets the wall is their usual entrance and exit route from the void spaces behind the wall. That is why pest control operators (PCOs), as they are called, spray along there as well as the garbage can area under the kitchen sink. Food crumbs and cookie crumbs provide a feeding site there. However pesticides should not be used where food is kept. This is too dangerous and should not be done by the do it yourselfers or by the PCOs that come into your home.

A better and safer way to manage food in the kitchen is to keep food stored inside plastic containers to prevent the cockroaches from getting to the food. Clean up all food crumbs on the kitchen counter top at night. The right designed garbage can inside the house for food scraps and recyclables should be made of plastic with a lid that prevents access by ants, cockroaches, and flies. That one thing alone, the right kitchen garbage can, goes a long way in keeping cockroaches at their lowest levels inside the home. Doorways can provide a pathway for cockroaches to enter the house from the outside. Windows and loose fitting window screens can also be pathways for cockroaches to enter the home as well as the sliding glass door. A liquid pyrethrin spray can be applied once a month to these areas. The product comes in a half gallon hand pumpsprayer for the home owner to use. Spray on the outside if possible and use as little as possible inside the house. This provides an effective barrier which the cockroaches will not cross. Pyrethrin products are safe if used correctly inside the home. They are the most repellent product for cockroaches that is available (See list of suppliers in the appendix). Spray the pyrethrin product along baseboards at the floor and wall junction.

Place boric acid powder product in the cracks and crevices along the junction of the floor and wall if you do not use the pyrethrin product there. A very light dusting only in areas where children and pets can not come in contact with the powder like behind the refrigerator and beside the stove. If a pet gets it on them wash it off with soap and water. Boric acid does not hurt the pet until they ingest it by licking it off their fur. All pesticide products should be kept in a locked cabinet along with other products that could be harmful to children if they ingest them (such as soaps and other cleaning fluids and products).

Caulking around any water pipes coming up thru the floor under the sink in the kitchen is a way of preventing cockroaches from entering the house. Caulking material is a putty like material that comes in a tube or can available at hardware stores or building supply stores. Also caulk around any pipes leading from outside the house to the inside as this prevents any insect from entering the house from the outside. As the person on the T.V. says "When in doubt CAULK." around all pipes and electrical wires as well as gas line pipes. Anything that provides a pathway into the house. Of course be careful around electric wiring. Before you caulk around a wire be sure to disconnect the electricity by removing the fuse at the fuse box.

Mopping the kitchen floor with Borax clothes washing powder followed by a clear water rinse once a month can be an effective way to lay down the Borax crystals near the floor and wall junction. A stronger product for commercial kitchens and restaurants can be used safely in the home. The trade name of the product is MOP-UP from R-VALUE/Waterbury Company, see appendix). The crystal salts of BORAX dry out after mopping and when the cockroach walks across the crystals, they cling to its legs. The cockroach runs its legs thru its mandibles or mouth and ingests the Borax. This kills the insect. The hairs on the legs of the cockroach and the crystals of the BORAX attract one another by static electric forces and by surface contact. The boric acid powder is not repellent to the cockroach and it does not react to it. The roach's reaction to the powder is presumably no different than its reaction to ordinary dirt particles. Therefore this is one of the best products to use on roaches.

Pyrethrin products, especially pyrethrin dust products, on the other hand, are one of the most repellent products and will cause cockroaches to run around wildly. Some PCOs put down the boric powder and then apply the pyrethrin product. This is suppose to cause the roaches to run across the boric acid powder and get it on them. Apply boric acid powder once a month or when trap monitoring indicates an increase in the population.

Home owners need to learn how to monitor cockroaches with glue boards because cockroaches come out at night. A glue board is just a flat piece of paper or cardboard with a thin layer of adhesive on it. The insects walk across it and get stuck. The adhesive has been specially formulated not to be repellent to the cockroach. They are available from pest control suppliers listed in the back of this book, or ask your local retail store if they carry them. Home made glue board traps can be made with a piece of notebook paper and "tanglefoot" or "stickem" product spread very thinly with a knife on an area of 3 inches by 6 inches. Place the paper on a counter top over night an see how many roaches are trapped in the morning. You should do this before you apply any pest control product then repeat after two weeks to see if the level of trapped insects is decreasing over time. Also doing this monitoring once a month will let the home owner know if an increase in population levels has occurred and the need to reapply a product before levels of cockroaches get too high. Most owners do not recognize the need to do this on a monthly basis but may be surprised to find that they either have a problem they do not know about or no problem at all. It is the only way to know if the materials and their application have worked. It also saves money and precludes the unnecessary use of any product or over use of a product. The glue boards can also be used to monitor for fleas and ticks inside the house.

References:
(1) See additional reading section and bibliography in the back of this book.
(2) See "Cockroaches" in next section of this book

Common Pests
of Gardens and Houses

The most troublesome pests tend to be insects, so they predominate this list. Since this is a book for gardeners, most of the pests are plant feeding types that plague gardens, but some house pests are also included. Controls listed may also be used for flowers, shrubs and fruit trees. Many insects feed and reproduce on other plants besides those in the garden.

All pests are presented in alphabetical order with the Latin name following the common name to help you if you'd like to research them further. In some instances many different species of an insect can be found, but the most common variety is listed. The drawings are meant to be representative of the insect form you will most likely encounter.

We describe the pests briefly with biological, cultural and acute controls. Acute controls should only be used when you need drastic help fast, since they may also kill beneficial organisms and upset the balance of nature. The use of long term biological or cultural control for prevention is better.

Insect Anatomy and Life Cycles

Adult insects have a head with two antennae, a thorax (in the middle), and an abdomen, with six legs on the thorax and usually, but not always, with a pair or two of wings, also on the thorax. Insect eggs usually hatch into larvae, also called caterpillars, grubs, maggots or worms. They transform into the adult form, a fly, butterfly or beetle after going through a pupal or cocoon stage. Other insects have eggs that hatch into nymphs that gradually transform into adult bugs. We describe in detail the life form that usually causes the gardener's direct problem. When lengths are given in inches, these are maximum lengths. The newly hatched insects are usually minute, almost, microscopic, but grow rapidly.

Ants *Formicidae family, hymenoptera order*

Fire Ants *Solenopsis geminata*

Ants live in colonies (hills, mounds) with queens that lay eggs. The wingless ones we most often see are sterile female workers. Most colonies are located in the soil. All attempts at ant control should be directed at the colony. Fire ants build small to large hills in pastures, fields and yards. The sting of a fire ant burns much more painfully than that of other ants. Currently, fire ants are generally limited to the Southeastern US. Their further spread will hopefully be limited by climate, but some regions of the Southwest may also be invaded. Mutations to a darker black color have already occurred among the black variety.

All ants have a very narrow junction between their thorax and abdomen. Ant colors vary from black to brown and red.

Life Cycle: 1. Eggs. 2. Larvae. 3. Pupa. 4. Adult, either Queen, worker or male. Sometimes there is more than one egg-laying queen per hill. New queens and males are constantly being raised. They are winged and fly away from the hill to form new colonies. An average colony can number 100,000 members and be found as deep into the ground as three feet. For fire ants a good time to apply some controls is during the colder months of the year when ants are less active.

Controls

Biological: *Pyemotes tritici*, or straw mite, is a predatory mite which is a naturally occurring predator of fire ants. They are commercially available. They also attack a wide variety of beetle larvae and caterpillars and many true bugs. Use a special strain of Nc nematode to kill fire ant colonies (see list of suppliers in appendix). Apply 1 - 2 million in a water suspension or on a carrier to the center of a colony at dusk. Wash in with 1 - 2 more quarts of water. Ant lions, the larval stage of brown lacewings or doodle bugs, eat ants but are not yet commercially available.

Cultural: Good aphid control helps control ants in the garden. Interplant spearmint, tansy and pennyroyal in the garden. Bone meal around the plants or juice of hot pepper pods on plants may act as a repellent.

Acute: A mixture of 3 to 4 tablespoons of liquid dish washing soap and ¼ cup.

of lime per gallon of water can be poured into a colony, 2 to 5 gallons at a time. After first drenching the center and perimeter of the hill, use a stick to probe deeply and uncover the center of the hill. Repeated applications may be necessary for larger hills. Since new queens fly in from other areas, yearly maintenance is necessary. An alternative control is to mix 1 million or less nematodes per 2-5 gallons of soapy drench. In the home, use soap and lime spray or pyrethrin dust or spray directly on the ants. *Ringer Crawling Insect Attack* provides good contact control with no residue. Place sugar or peanut butter as a bait to determine the location of the colony. Boric Acid, which is $NaBO$, sodium borate, mixed with a mint-apple jelly (trade name *Drax*) is the most preferred product for ants in the kitchen. Notice the similarity to salt, $NaCl$. In fact, both are found in large surface deposits near one another in California.

Aphids or Plant Lice *Aphidae family, homoptera order (4,000 species)*

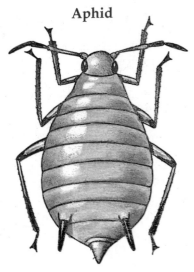

Aphid

Aphids are ¹/₁₀ to ½ inch long pear shaped bugs with or without wings. They are soft bodied and can be green, yellow or black. They are usually found on the underside of new leaves and along tender plant shoots. Here they pierce plants and suck juices. Ants guard the aphids from other insects and eat the gooey honeydew, which aphids excrete. Winged forms and male aphids usually appear around autumn.

Life Cycle: 1. Egg on leaf. 2. Hatch to nymph stage (small adult form). 3. Adults feed on leaves and lay eggs.

Controls

Biological: Ladybug beetles and their larvae, lacewings and their larvae and aphid midges (*aphidoletes aphidimyza*) all eat aphids and aphid eggs.

Cultural: Fall plowing helps kill overwintering aphid eggs outdoors. Inter plant mint.

Acute: Hose off plants with water. Once disturbed aphids may not return. Dust wet plants heavily with lime or spray plants with lime and water solution. Use homemade soap spray alone or lime and soap spray together. *Ringer Aphid-Mite Attack Insecticidal Soap* provides good control. *Safer™ Insecticidal Soap* and *Chevron-Ortho Insecticidal Soap* are available. Also newer horticultural oils like *Sunspray* smother aphids and aphid eggs.

31

Apple Maggots *Rhagoletis pomonella*

These yellow-white legless larvae bore into apples after hatching from eggs laid into punctures made by the parent flies. The mature maggots fall to the ground, pupate and winter over. They can be found throughout the US.

Controls

Biological: Apply Nc nematodes as a soil top dressing in the late summer to early fall to kill maggots as they fall to the ground. Place plastic apples or solid red and yellow balls together in the trees in and near the orchard, smeared with tanglefoot or another sticky substance in the spring and summer to trap adults. Commercial traps are also available.

Cultural: Pick up and use or destroy all apples as they fall.

Armyworms *Euxoa auxiliaris and several other species*
Fall Armyworms *Spodoptera frugiperda and several other species*

This greenish two inch long caterpillar with yellow stripes down its back is actually a type of cutworm feeding near the ground, often on stalks. Its gray moth lays eggs on grasses and corn. The night feeding worms eat that grass until they grow larger, then as their food runs out they "march" to other plants looking for food. The "fall armyworm" has a similar biology but comes in a variety of colors and doesn't leave host plants during the day. Fall army-

Armyworm

worm moths fly north from the southern US every spring.

Life Cycle: 1. Eggs laid on leaves. 2. Larva feeds on grass and stems on ground at night in the early spring and later feeds on plants and leaves. 3. Pupates in soil. 4. Adult butterfly.

Controls

Biological: Use trichogramma, lacewings, and beneficial Nc nematodes as a soil mulch. Spray or dust Bt or NPV on plants. Handpick in soil near plant.

Cultural: Control weeds, mow grass, interplant strong smelling herbs, fall plowing.

Acute: Use Nc nematodes and Bt. Spray soap and lime directly on caterpillars. Use commercial pheromone traps for monitoring and low level trapping out of adult stage moth. Homemade light traps using funnel design for night flying moths can also be used.

Bagworms *Thyridopteryx ephemeraeformis*

Bagworm

These pests are "wolves in sheep's clothing," pests that disguise themselves with parts of the arbor vitae, cedar or other shrubs or foliage they eat. Inside the spindle-shaped bag formed of leaf parts that they glue to together with silk are dirty brown caterpillars. They drag their bags along as they feed. A horde of bagworms can easily defoliate and kill a tree. Most are found east of the Mississippi River.

Life Cycle: 1. Eggs laid in the bag winter over and hatch in early spring. 2. Larva. 3. Pupa in late summer. 4. Adult butterfly.

Controls

Biological: With light infestations handpicking bags is effective. Use Bt.

Acute: For heavier infestations spray Bt on foliage. Avoid chemical contact poisons which kill naturally occurring parasitic wasps. Malathion, for example, has a residency period of 30 days and a negative effect on wasps like trichogramma due to fumes and vapor. This invites reinfestation.

Bean Leaf Beetles *Cerotoma trifurcata*

These are ¼ inch long and reddish with 4 black spots and a black head. Their eggs are laid on leaves. The larvae enter the soil and feed on roots. Adult beetles feed on leaves.

Life Cycle: 1. Eggs on leaves. 2. Larvae enter soil. 3. Pupa. 4. Adults feed on leaves.

Controls

Biological: Ladybug beetles and lacewings eat eggs. As an experiment for killing larvae and emerging adults, mix beneficial nematodes into seed furrow and use as a mulch around plants. Handpick bugs off plants and destroy.

Bean Leaf Beetle

33

Cultural: Interplant potatoes, garlic, cloves and radishes along with beans. Fall plowing helps destroy eggs.

Acute: Spray garlic, onion or pepper extract to repel or soap and lime spray on beetle to irritate. Spot spray rotenone or a pyrethrin product.

Blackflies *Simulium damnosum and other species*
These ¹⁄₂₅ to ¹⁄₅ inch gnats are a nuisance to gardeners. They bite around the head and arms, suck blood, then lays eggs in moving, well oxygenated water. The eggs hatch into bowling pin shaped black maggots that attach to stones and bottom debris in streams. Usually there is only one generation per year, but even a small stream can produce millions of blackflies each spring. Biting species can have 3-4 generations per year.

Controls

Biological: For control the following spring, apply Bti rings upstream or spray Bti in the late summer or early fall. Bti is a special strain of Bt which only affects blackfly and mosquito larvae.

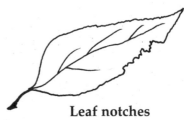

Black Vine Weevils
Otiorrhynchus sulcatus
This shy night feeding weevil eats notches on the sides of the leaves of yew tree (*taxus*), rhododendron bushes, aza- **Leaf notches**
leas. and other ornamental shrubs. It lays eggs in soil. The eggs hatch into white legless grubs which feed on roots and kill plants. During the day weevils remain well concealed in mulch and leaf litter on the ground. The leaf notches are the surest signs of this serious pest.

Controls

Biological: Use insect eating nematodes in a mulch around bushes. Hoe in around roots. Applying tanglefoot around trunk of the bushes or trees will prevent adults from climbing and eating leaves.

Cultural: Be sure to buy uninfested nursery stock. Prune lower branches that are in contact with the ground.

Blister Beetles *Epicauta pestifera (several other species)*

These are solid black flying beetles, sometimes black with yellow stripes. They are ½ inch long with long legs and a narrow neck. They cause skin to blister if handled. They eat leaves, fruit and stems, but their larvae are all beneficial and prey on grasshopper eggs, so you might want to leave them alone.

Life Cycle: 1. Eggs laid in soil. 2. Larvae in soil. 3. Pupa in soil. 4. Adult beetle.

Controls

Biological: Hand pick with gloves or use   **Blister Beetle**
broom to move large populations away from
your garden. Experiment with Nc nematodes in hay pastures and grass yards for larval stage control.

Acute: Dust wet plants heavily with lime or use lime spray to cause them to leave the garden. Use soap and lime spray if all else fails. Spot spray a pyrethrin or rotenone product on plants.

Cabbage Loopers *Trichoplusia ni*

This white striped green caterpillar forms a loop with its body when it crawls. Its nocturnal moth lays single eggs on leaves and is brownish in color.

Life Cycle: 1. Eggs on leaves. 2. Larva eats leaves. 3. Pupa. 4. Adult butterfly.

Cabbage Looper

Controls

Biological: Release trichogramma and lacewings for preventative control. For quicker control, dust or spray Bt or NPV.

Cultural: Interplant strong smelling herbs to deter butterfly or moth egg laying. Handpick caterpillar off plant. Fall plow.

Acute: Dust wet plant with lime or spray with soap and lime. Spray with Bt or NPV if labeled for loopers. Use Nc as a spray on plants. Apply late in the day.

Root Maggots *Hylemya brassicae*

These legless white maggots with a black "hook" in their heads attack the roots of cabbage, broccoli, cauliflower, radishes, turnips and some other plants. Similar maggots attack carrots and onions. Often their attack will rot the whole root or the plants die. Plants set in the fall can also be attacked. Two generations may occur per year.

Life Cycle: 1. Eggs laid in soil crevices 2. Larva (maggot) in plant roots 3. Pupa in soil 4. Adult fly hatches in early spring

Controls

Biological: Apply beneficial Nc nematodes at planting in seed furrow or around transplants.

Cultural: Crop rotation, never plant susceptible plants within flying distance of areas planted in the last two years.

Acute: Use Nc nematodes or lime spray or dust on ground around plants to deter egg laying.

Chinch Bugs *Blissus leucopterus*

This ⅛ to ⅕ inch black bug with white, red or brown wings feed on grasses and corn. The adults hibernate in grass then lay eggs in the soil in the spring. These hatch into reddish wingless nymphs. In about 30-40 days they turn into adult bugs and produce another generation. The grains and grasses they attack look brown and dried out, caused by the nymphs and adults sucking sap.

Chinch Bug

Life cycle: 1. Eggs in soil. 2. Nymph (small adult). 3. Adults that winter over in grass.

Controls

Biological: As an experiment use beneficial Nc nematodes applied as a soil top dressing or mulch. They may attack adults and nymphs as they hide on the ground or in grass. Keep ground moist. Ladybug beetles and lacewings provide some control.

Cultural: Use fall plowing. Clean up weed and brush where adults winter over.

Acute: Use soap spray to kill bugs or spray garlic, onion and pepper extract to repel them. Use soap spray on heavily infested lawns.

Cockroaches *Blattella germanica*
There are four main North American species of this house pest. They eat everything that humans eat plus some of what we can't or won't, such as paper. They thrive in moist, warm and dark environments.

Controls

Cultural: Dry houses in colder climates with floors that are crevice-free can deter cockroaches. In other situations, good sanitation is a must. Clean up food and dishes at night and take care of any damp areas. Keep garbage cans and food sealed in metal or thick plastic. Seal the house with tight fitting screens and doors. Seal around pipes leading outside with caulking material. Seal around window screens and doorways if necessary.

Acute: Use boric acid powder, trade name *Roach Kil*™ or *Roach Proof*™ or a similar product. Most people over-apply this product. A very light fine dusting near cracks and crevices where roaches walk is all that's needed. Boric acid bait stations, trade name *It Works*, are available in a plastic child proof enclosure. A boric acid product to use in mop water, called *Mop-Up*, is commercially available. Keep boric acid powder products stored away from children. Do not use the powder where pets can get it on them. **Boric acid is a poison.** It is very long lasting and should be the number one product for roach control in the house. See Additional Reading Section in the back of this book for more information on roach control. See especially "IPM for Home and Garden" and Least Toxic Roach Control from the publishers of "IPM Practitioner" and the "Common Sense Pest Control Quarterly."

Codling Moth Larvae *Laspeyresia pomonella*
This pink, or white tinged with pink caterpillar is the proverbial worm in the apple. Without some kind of control. most apples get them.

Life Cycle: Two or three generations per year, occurring every 5-8 weeks.
1. Emerging moths lay eggs on leaves, twigs and buds. 2. Larva enters the apple, grows, emerges and climbs down tree trunk. 3. Pupates either under loose bark, in trash.

Codling Moth Larva

on the ground or other protected area. The third generation larva winters over, then pupates in early spring. 4. Emerging moth, butterfly, lays eggs. Moth emergence is extended throughout the spring, summer and fall, but has three distinct peaks.

Controls

Biological: Timed release of trichogramma at the three peaks of egg laying. Begin spring release at petal fall, then release 3-8 weeks later in summer, and 5-8 weeks after that in early fall. Timing releases is important, so it helps to monitor traps. Spray wet tree trunks and underneath trees with Nc nematodes. A late winter spray is most effective before the larvae pupate. Respray three weeks after petal fall, then again after another four weeks or whenever you collect fresh larvae in the cardboard trap. Wrap trunks with several thicknesses of corrugated cardboard one foot or so in length. Remove larvae weekly. Gently scrape loose bark off tree each spring and fall and destroy.

Cultural: Fall cleanup, remove fallen apples, trash and leaves and bum or compost leaves. Interplant clover as a ground cover, and flowers, such as daisies or other field flowers. Plant only disease resistant apple varieties like "Liberty" and "Freedom" that are for your geographic area.

Acute: No acute spray, chemical or otherwise is effective once the worm is in the apple. Spray codling moth virus at petal fall, then at intervals determined by trap monitoring of adult moths. The object is to kill young larvae before they enter apples. Use lime and soap spray weekly on tree trunk and around base on larva. Spray entire tree with soap and lime spray before leaves appear and buds open in late winter (dormant stage spraying).

Colorado Potato Beetle

Colorado Potato Beetles
Leptinotarsa decemlineata
This round ⅜ inch yellow beetle with black stripes eats potato leaves and lays yellow-orange egg masses on the undersides of the leaves. The ½ inch reddish, humpbacked, legged grubs chew leaves and have black dots on their sides.

Life Cycle: Several generations can be completed per year. 1. Eggs on leaves. 2. Larva feed on leaves. 3. Pupa in soil. 4. Adults emerge after 10 days and eventually hibernate in the soil during the winter.

Controls

Biological: Release beneficial insect *Edovum puttleri*, lacewings and lady-bug beetles which eat eggs. Handpick eggs, larva and adults off plants. *Use Ringer Colorado Potato Beetle Attack* (Bt-sd) and others for control of early larval stage only.

Cultural: Interplant green beans with potatoes. Fall plow to kill adults.

Acute: Spray garlic, onion and pepper juice as a repellent or soap spray directly on the beetles to irritate them. Use soap and lime spray on larvae to kill them by dehydration.

Corn Earworm

Corn Earworms *Heliothis zea* **Cotton Bollworms** *H. zea* **Tobacco Budworms** *H. virescens* **Tomato Fruitworms** *H. zea*
The color of these 2 inch caterpillars varies from white, brown, and black-ish to red with stripes and hair tufts. They actually attack a variety of plants and have been called the tobacco budworm, cotton bollworm and tomato fruitworm.

Life Cycle: Several generations occur yearly. 1. Eggs are laid by the thou-sands on a variety of plants including corn, beans and tomatoes. 2. Larvae hatch and feed on leaves, then corn silk and kernels of the ear. 3. The caterpillars pupate in the soil 3-5 inches deep, emerging after 10-25 days. 4. Adult moth, the final generation wintering over in the pupal stage to emerge the following spring.

Controls

Biological: Release trichogramma and lacewings. Spread Nc nematodes on the ground as a mulch. Spray Nc on silks or inject onto silks with a medicine dropper at regular intervals. Spray Bt or NPV on leaves and silks. Handpick worms off leaves.

Cultural: Fall plowing destroys pupae in the soil. No lights should be left on near the garden at night to attract the moths.

Acute: See above for Nc, Bt and NPV, spraying weekly for complete con-trol or as needed.

Cowpea Curculios (Bean Weevils) *Acanthoscelides obtectus*
These are small black beetles with a snout. They lay eggs in pods. They are usually found on southern peas and lima beans.

Life Cycle: 1. Eggs laid inside pod. 2. Larva feed in pod. 3. Pupate in pod. 4. Adult emerges.

Controls

Biological: As an experiment try nematodes as a soil mulch around plants as a possible control. A praying mantis may eat several adults. Use nematodes around over wintering sites of adult stage, such as wood piles or cracks and crevices in the greenhouse.

Cultural: Use fall plowing and interplant garlic, cloves, potatoes and radishes. Place a sheet or cloth beneath plants and shake gently. Weevils should fall on the sheet. Gather and destroy by crushing or dropping in alcohol. Dry seeds thoroughly and turn or shake once a week, leaving an opening for adults to escape. They will look for a less disrupted resting place.

Acute: Use garlic, onion and pepper spray on pods to deter egg laying. Use lime and soap spray on adult weevils as an irritant.

Cucumber Beetles Striped *Acalymma vittatum (Syn. Diabrotica vittatum)* **Spotted** *Diabrotica undecimpunctata howardi*

These are green or yellow beetles with three black stripes or 12 black dots They winter over, then emerge to spread diseases and eat leaves. They feed on cucumbers and related plants, such as melons and squash. The larva are ½ inch long with a dark head.

Life Cycle: Two generations may occur per year in warm climates. 1. Eggs around the bases of the plants and in cracks in the soil. 2. The legged larvae feed in the stems and roots. The larval stage is also called cornrootworm. 3. Pupate in soil. 4. Adult beetle.

Spotted Cucumber Beetle

Controls

Biological: Lacewings and ladybug beetles eat eggs. Apply beneficial Nc nematodes as a mulch around plants to kill adults. Apply around roots of transplants or in seed furrow at planting time to kill larvae. Handpick bugs.

Cultural: Interplant radishes, fall plow and use crop rotation.

Acute: Spray plants with lime to deter beetle feeding or soap and lime spray directly on the beetle to irritate and possibly kill them. Use pyrethrin or sabadilla dust.
Caution: sabadilla dust may cause allergic reaction if inhaled. Use dust mask. Certain rotenone products are useful.

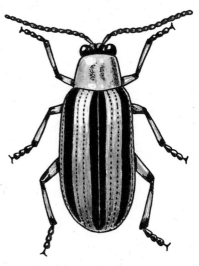

Striped Cucumber Beetle

Cutworms *Noctuidae family, lepidoptera order (various species)*

There are several species of cutworms. Some are glassy green, others are whitish, brown or black. Some are striped or banded. They feed on a variety of garden plants, including corn, beans, cabbage and numerous others. Many cutworms cut off plants at the base of the stems feeding little, but doing much damage, while many others climb up plants and strip leaves. All these caterpillars tend to feed and move on the soil surface at night. In the day they often lay curled up on or near the soil surface like a "c" near the plants they attack. Some cutworms start behaving like armyworms when food is exhausted.

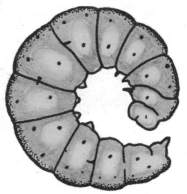

Life Cycle: In the south several generations occur per year. 1. Eggs are laid on plant stems or on bare ground near plants. 2. Larva or worm stage, wintering over buried in the soil. 3. Pupate in the spring. 4. Adult moth. Some species overwinter in pupal stage.

Cutworm

Controls

Biological: Trichogramma and lacewings attack eggs. Apply Nc beneficial nematodes as a mulch around plants. Handpick from soil around plants.

Cultural: Use fall plowing or plow repeatedly before planting. Wrap individual foil or paper collars around stems of plants. Turn off lights near garden at night. Place a piece of sandpaper or a piece of roofing shingle on the ground around plants. The caterpillars will not crawl across the rough surfaces.

Acute: Spread Nc nematodes. Bt spray is effective for strippers. Use Bt spray on the ground and stem to give some help in controlling stem cutters.

Diamond-back moth larvae *Plutella xylostella*
This is a thin green ⅙ inch long caterpillar with a black head. It hangs from a silken thread and eats holes in plant leaves. The moth is gray to yellow in color with a diamond shaped area formed at the tail end of the wings when the wings are folded and it is viewed from the side.

Controls
Same as for imported cabbage worm

Earwigs *Forficula auricularia*
These ¾ inch brownish black wingless insects look scary, but do not pinch people with the forceps-like pincers on their abdomens. Since many prey upon aphids and other pests, they are more beneficial than harmful. They like confined areas, are active at night and feed on decayed plant material. Because they kill a pest, clean up the decay it has caused and hide there, we often accuse them of doing the damage to the plant. It would be a mistake to over-react and spray for them. Adult earwigs tend the eggs laid in the soil, then watch over the young nymphs like ducks watching their young until they are able to feed themselves.

Earwig

Life Cycle: 1. Eggs winter over in soil. 2. Nymph stage. 3. Adult.

Cultural: Trap them in rolled up newspaper or something else they can hide in. Move to another area. They seek cool protected areas during the day.

Acute: Use insecticidal soap spray directly on the adults.

Eastern Tent Caterpillars *Malacosoma americanum*
These dark caterpillars have a white stripe on their backs and yellow and brown lines and blue spots on their sides. The tent-like webs they spin may be a more distinctive characteristic. They eat the leaves of a variety of fruit and shade trees, except for evergreens. Tent caterpillars widely occur east of the Rockies in the US and southern Canada.

Life Cycle: 1. Eggs, laid in masses that encircle twigs, hatch in the spring. 2. Larva eats leaves. 3. Pupae winter over in trash or bark. 4. Adult moth.

Biological: Release trichogramma and lacewings. Spray Bt on foliage when caterpillars are feeding on leaves.

Eastern Tent Caterpillar

Cultural: Good fall clean-up of leaves, twigs limbs and fallen fruit and nuts. Remove web tents and kill all caterpillars. Use strong stream of water to tear up tents high up in tall trees. Interplant flowers and clover.

Acute: Use Bt spray on leaves or soap and lime spray directly on caterpillars.

European Corn Borer *Ostrinia nubilalis*
These one inch gray-pink caterpillars with brown spots are found boring in corn or a variety of grasses.

Life Cycle: Several generations may occur per year. 1. Egg masses on undersides of leaves. 2. Small larvae that feed first on leaves, then bore into stalks. 3. Pupa. 4. Nocturnally active adult moths, pupa winter over in bore holes.

Controls

European Corn Borer

Biological: Trichogramma, ladybug beetles and lacewings all attack eggs. Squirt or spray Nc nematodes into borehole. Bt can be sprayed before borers enter the stalk, but this has limited effectiveness.

Cultural: Fall plowing destroys overwintering forms. Resistant corn varieties are available.

Acute: Cut a slit in the stalk and remove borer. Use light traps and pheromone traps for monitoring and low level trapping out.

Fleas *Ctenocephalides felis. canis.*
Ticks
The wingless adult fleas are blood-sucking parasites of animals. Their eggs are deposited in dirt, dust, the bedding of their host or carpet.

Life Cycle: Can vary from 2 to 12 weeks, and can be as long as 2 years 1. Eggs. 2. Larva. 3. Pupa. 4. Adult flea.

Controls

Biological: Beneficial Nc nematodes attack flea larvae in turf. Keep it moist. *Hunterellus hookeri* is a tick parasite. Use a white canvas drag sheet to monitor tick levels.

Cultural: Inside vacuuming sucks up eggs, larvae and pupae at the same time it removes flea food. Clean pet bedding frequently. Clean up animal refuse outside.

Acute: Use pyrethrin-based flea collars, pet shampoos and soaps on dogs. Sprinkle pyrethrin-based flea powder on carpet followed by vacuuming and/or rug shampooing. Remove and dispose of vacuum bag immediately after vacuuming. In the yard, spray or dust a pyrethrin or rotenone product. Use on animal refuse. **Caution:** pyrethrin products should not be used on cats due to allergic skin reaction. Use rotenone or pyrethrin spray outside on heavily tick infested areas such as picnic sites. A parasite of ticks should be released for more permanent control. See *Least Toxic Flea and Tick Control* from "IPM Practitioner".

Flea Beetles *Phyllotreta striolata*

A jumping beetle, ¼ inch or less, sometimes with black and yellow stripes. They eat tiny holes in young leaves. Larvae feed on seeds and roots.

Life Cycle: 1. Eggs in soil. 2. Larva in soil. 3. Pupa. 4. Adult beetle.

Controls

Biological: Apply beneficial Nc nematodes in seed furrow and as a mulch around plants.

Cultural: Use good weed control and repeated early spring cultivation along with fall plowing. Interplant mint.

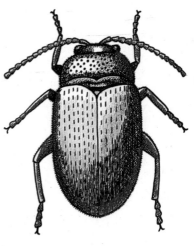

Flea Beetle

Acute: Use garlic, onion and pepper spray as a repellent. Heavily dust wet plants and the wet ground around plants with lime, lime spray or soap and lime spray. **Caution:** do not overuse lime. It could change the soil Ph.

Flies, (including house fly and other filth fly species) *Musca domestica*

Various species of these flies all require fresh excrement from a warm blooded animal to complete their life cycle. Needless to say, they can spread disease. Others bite and suck blood or suck tears.

Life Cycle: In hot weather, cycle can take only a couple of weeks. 1. Cylindrical eggs in fresh manure. 2. Legless maggots with a black hook on their heads. 3. Pupate in a drier area, pupa has a brown, leathery shell. 4. Adult fly emerges in several days.

Controls

Biological: Introduce fly parasites each year on a weekly basis near fresh and dry manure. These parasites deposit their eggs in fly pupae. They are commercially available for use around dairies, chicken houses, feed mills, stables, barns, etc.

Cultural: Clean out fresh manure every three days and allow to dry. Dry manure harbors fly parasites so leave about 8 inches of the dry manure base. Eliminate water leaks or continuously moist areas.

Acute: If adult fly populations get out of hand, use pyrethrin aerosol spray or fly traps. Do not use around fly parasite breeding areas. Keep pyrethrin away from water and animal feed and bedding. Do not spray inside the barn.

Grasshoppers *Acrididae family, orthoptera order (various species)*

Various species of 1 to 2 inch grasshoppers chew on almost all wild and cultivated plants. Many are gray-brown-green.

Life Cycle: 1. Egg masses laid in soil. 2. Wingless nymphs hatch the next year. 3. Winged adult develop by summer.

Controls

Biological: Praying mantis may eat grasshoppers. The beneficial protozoan *Nosema locustae* controls most species of grasshoppers and some crickets. It is sold as *Grasshopper Attack* and several other brand names. If you live in an area plagued by grasshoppers, you will get quickest benefits by applying it as a preventative by early summer every other year when the nymphs are small. The effect of this treatment will be optimal the next summer.

Cultural: Fall plowing destroys eggs, but grasshoppers often lay eggs in rough, unplowable areas.

Acute: Spray soap directly on the grasshoppers. As an experiment, mix some nematodes with the soap spray and apply late in the evening or at night.

Gypsy Moth Larvae *Lymantria dispar*

These gray caterpillars are two inches long with tufts of brown and yellow hair extending from its sides and with 10 blue spots followed by 12 red spots on its back. Thousands of them can be found in a tree, which they will defoliate and kill, if it's attacked more than once. They don't spin webs or tents in the foliage. The caterpillars often migrate down a tree trunk in the day and return up the trunk at night to feed. If a tree is defoliated they may abandon it, "march" over the ground and attack a wide variety of other plants. The caterpillars also migrate down tree trunks to spin a loose cocoon and form dark leathery pupae. Currently they occur from New England to West Virginia, but are spreading south and west. Localized infestations have been found in Illinois and Oregon. In areas where the gypsy moth is established, heavy outbreaks occur every fourth year when parasites get naturally out of balance.

Life Cycle: 1. Large brown egg masses on trunk, branches, rocks, ground, bark and trash. 2. Larvae hatch in spring, climb to top of tree and release long strands of silk that catch the wind and help transport the caterpillars many miles. 3. Pupa or cocoon stage. 4. Adult moth, males are gray, white females cannot fly.

Controls

Biological: Lacewings may attack eggs. Other commercially available parasites sites are *Glyptapanteles Flavicoxis* and *Cotesia Melanoscelus*. The moth scales on the egg masses seem to prevent Trichogramma attack. Apply Nc nematode as a top dressing around tree trunks to kill migrating caterpillars. Spray foliage with Bt or NPV onto leaf surfaces at the first sign of a massive infestation to kill the smaller more susceptible larvae.

Cultural: Tie a rope around tree trunk, then drape a burlap cloth over the rope. Remove caterpillars that gather there daily or spray cloth with Nc nematodes and keep moist. Handpick pupae. Scrape off and destroy egg masses. Practice good fall clean-up of leaves and limbs around trees.

Acute: Use Bt or NPV spray on leaves when caterpillars are feeding. You can use a water hose and quart attachment, but be sure to use a back flow preventor on the hose to prevent water with microbes from flowing back into the house plumbing system. These microbes are harmless to humans but it is a good practice not to ingest them. Use lime and soap spray on caterpillars and eggs. Spay Nc on wet tree trunks and the ground around trees.

Gypsy Moth Larva

Head Lice *Pediculosis humanus capitis*

A wingless parasitic insect about ¹⁄₁₀ inch long that bites and sucks blood from the scalp of the host person, causing itchy swelling. It lays eggs, also called nits, to strands of hair.

Life Cycle: 1. Egg (Nit). 2. Nymph. 3. Adult.

Controls

Shampoo head with coconut oil shampoo and use a head lice comb to remove egg cases from hair shaft. Repeat as necessary or use a shampoo with pyrethrin in it available at drug stores. For persistent infestations, the best remedy is to remove the eggs or nits by hand. This is best done in good sunlight or under a strong light source by someone other than the person with the infestation. Shampoo hair as directed above and dry. Divide the hair into small sections and examine each strand, stripping down the hair with your fingernails to pull off the nit. Be sure to carefully collect and dispose of the nits as they are found. Repeat this process daily until no eggs have been seen for several days. This is a time consuming but dependable method. See suggested literature in the appendix for more information. For more information see literature from "IPM Practitioner" or National Pediculosis Association, P.O. Box 149, Newton, MA 02161.

Harlequin Bugs *Murgantia histrionica*

These black and red or black and yellow ½ inch shield shaped bugs suck plant juices. The winged adults lay tiny barrel shaped eggs in rows or masses on the undersides of leaves. Harlequin bugs winter over in trash or leaves as adults or nymphs.

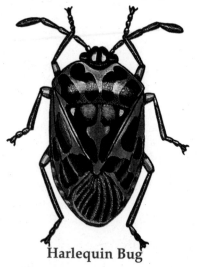

Life Cycle: 1. Eggs. 2. Nymph or small adult stage. 3. Adult.

Controls

Biological: Handpick bugs and eggs. Praying mantis may eat bugs and nymphs. As an experiment, use *pymotes*. **Caution:** use only in an area away from homes, livestock and people, not in a home garden. If *pymotes* get out of hand, use soap spray.

Cultural: Use fall plowing and control weeds.

Harlequin Bug

Acute: Use insect soap spray.

Imported Cabbage Worm *Pieris rapae*

The green one inch long caterpillar with a yellow stripe on its back eats leaves. Its white butterfly is active in the day and lays several hundred eggs on leaves. This butterfly has a 1¼ inch wingspan with dark spots on its wings.

Life Cycle: 1. Eggs. 2. Larva eats leaves. 3. Pupa or cocoon stage. 4. Adult butterfly.

Imported Cabbage Worm

Controls

Biological: Generally same controls for all caterpillars. Release trichogramma and lacewings. Spray or dust Bt or NPV. Handpick larvae off plant and use a butterfly net to catch moths. Use *Apantales rubecula*, a braconid wasp, to be released for permanent establishment in the environment.

Cultural: Interplant rosemary and thyme or sage.

Acute: Spray or dust with Bt or NPV. Use soap and lime spray directly on caterpillar. Dust wet plants with lime. Spray with soap and lime three consecutive days before harvest to kill new worms.

Japanese Beetles *Popillia japonica*

The metallic blue or green adult beetles with coppery wing covers feed on foliage and flowers. In June to August they enter the soil to lay eggs which hatch into white, comma-shaped grubs with six legs. Like other species of white grubs, they feed on tender roots, most often grass. Japanese beetle grubs are the most common white grubs in Eastern US, but often other species predominate locally. All species of white grubs destroy lawns, leaving large brown areas that turn brown and peel back like a rug when pulled. They winter over in the soil and pupate there the next June.

Japanese Beetle

Life Cycle: 1. Eggs laid in soil. 2. Larva feed on grass roots. 3. Pupate in soil. 4. Adults leave soil as beetles.

Controls

Biological: Apply Nc nematodes as top dressing in spring. Apply milky spore disease, *Bacillus popilliae*, to lawns, grassy areas and fruit orchards. Leave some places untreated for grubs so there will be some for the birds.

Cultural: Interplant garlic and larkspur to repel beetles. Use spike aerator sandals on lawns in late spring to kill larval stage of **all** beetle grubs. They are feeding near the surface at this time.

Acute: Dust or spray pyrethrin. Spray garlic, onion and pepper mixture to deter adult feeding. Handpick adults. Spray soap and lime directly on the bugs to irritate them.

Leafminers *Liriomyza sp.*

After the parent flies lay eggs on leaf surfaces, the newly hatched maggots burrow in. Green or black ⅛ inch maggots tunnel between the upper and lower leaf surfaces leaving a white trail behind them.

Life Cycle: Three or four generations of flies can hatch per year. 1. Eggs laid on leaf surfaces. 2. Larvae tunnel into leaf. 3. Mature maggots fall to ground and pupate. 4. Adult fly.

Controls

Biological: Ladybug beetles and lacewings may eat eggs. Other parasites, *diglyphus begini* and *diglyphus isaea*, are commercially available.

Cultural: Remove and destroy infested leaves. Fall plowing destroys pupae. Covering plants with cheese cloth netting prevents egg laying. Rotate crops.

Acute: Spray hot pepper juice or lime spray. Dust wet plants heavily with lime to repel flies and deter egg laying.

Leaf Rollers *Lepidoptera order (various species)*
Several species of caterpillars, all spin a web in leaves and roll leaves to pupate in.

Life Cycle: 1. Eggs laid on stems. 2. Larva or caterpillar stage. 3. Pupa or cocoon stage. 4. Adult butterfly.

Controls

Biological: Release lacewings or trichogramma to destroy eggs. Spray Bt on foliage to kill caterpillars.

Cultural: Cut off and destroy infested leaves. Interplant strong herbs to discourage egg laying.

Acute: Bt spray on plant leaves. Use NPV or soap and lime spray directly on caterpillars.

Leafhoppers *Graphacephala coccinea (several other species)*
These slender ⅛ inch long wedge-shaped bugs suck plant juices, kill leaves and spread virus diseases of plants. There are several species. Some are all green. Others are green with red and white markings. All of them hop or fly when disturbed. Often they sit and feed on the undersides of leaves. They are pests on a variety of plants including apples, beets and potatoes. Dragonflies eat leafhoppers.

Life Cycle: 1. Eggs on plants, winter over. 2. Nymph (small adult). 3. Adult, some hibernate in trash, others migrate north in spring after wintering over in the south.

Controls

Biological: Lacewings eat eggs.

Cultural: Use fall plowing.

Leafhopper

Acute: Use insecticidal soap spray early in the morning when the insects are less active.

Lesser Corn Stalk Borers *Elasmopalpus lignosellus*
The green, blue or brown banded caterpillars tunnel into corn stems, usually near the soil surface and wriggle wildly when held. The caterpillar exits the stalk through a tube-like silken web and pupates in the soil. This pest may occur in other regions and damage other plants, but is worst in Southern corn.

Life Cycle: 1. Eggs on leaves. 2. Larva. 3. Pupa in soil. 4. Butterfly.

Controls

Biological: Beneficial Nc nematodes as a mulch or inject into the borehole. Release trichogramma, ladybugs and lacewings.

Cultural: Fall plow. Make a small cut on the stalk near bore hole and remove borer. Use crop rotation.

Acute: Use Bt and NPV sprays to provide some control before caterpillar enters stalk.

Mealybug *Pseudococcus adonidum*
Adults are elliptically shaped with short spines, actually a part of their waxy white covering. Females have no wings, do not move and no legs are visible. The males do not feed in this stage, but transform into a two-winged flier that mates with the immobile female, then dies. Eggs are laid within the waxy case and hatch into six-legged bugs with smooth bodies. These disperse, "stick" to the plant and begin sucking juices. Soon afterward, they secrete the white covering and after that only move sluggishly. They attack a wide variety of soft-stemmed foliage plants under greenhouse conditions. Here the life cycle takes about one month.

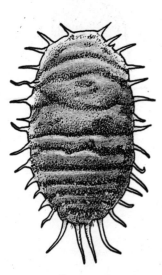

Life cycle: 1. Eggs laid in protected areas under bark. 2. Nymph (small adult). 3. Adult, ¼ inch in length.

Controls

Biological: Both the *Cryptolaemus* ladybug (not the common one) and *Pauridia* parasites are commercially available for use.

Mealybug

Cultural: Quarantine new potted plants for 30 days and examine weekly for mealybugs. In early spring spray dormant stage with soap.

Acute: Wash off with high pressure water, but be careful not to damage plants. Spray soap or touch individual insects with alcohol on a cotton swab. It may take repeated application.

Mexican Bean Beetles *Epilachna varivestis*
Light brown beetles with 16 black dots on their backs resemble ladybug beetles. They skeletonize bean leaves and lay yellow egg clusters on leaf undersides. Their yellow-orange larvae also feed on leaves.

Life Cycle: 1. Eggs on leaves. 2. Larva eat leaves. 3. Pupa. 4. Adult beetle.

Controls

Biological: Release parasite *Pediobius foveolatus*. Handpick bugs and eggs.

Cultural: Interplant potatoes, garlic, cloves, turnips, marigolds and radishes. Fall plowing helps control populations.

Acute: Garlic, onion and pepper juice spray will deter feeding. Use lime and soap spray as an irritant or pyrethrin to kill. Rotenone is labeled for Mexican Bean Beetles.

Mexican Bean Beetle

Moles
These furry, warm-blooded animals live underground. They tunnel, searching for grubs and worms. They don't eat roots, but the tunneling damages gardens and the yards.

Controls

Biological: You may want to plant four or five castor bean plants or "mole plant", *Euphobia lathyris*, in or near your garden. Both plants are somewhat poisonous. Do not allow small children to eat the leaves or stems.

Cultural: The major cause of mole activity in lawns and gardens is an excess of pest insects like white grubs. Control the grubs and the moles will leave the area.

Acute: Use commercially available spring loaded mole traps.

Mosquitoes *Culex pipiens (several other species)*

Female mosquitoes digest a blood meal, then lay eggs in water or on a surface that is regularly flooded. The water of mosquito development must be still. Eggs hatch into aquatic larvae (wrigglers) that feed on bacteria, then turn into pupae in the same water. In hot weather the adults emerge in several days. For certain species there is only one generation per year, but there are multiple generations of some species in most of North America.

For information on area-wide program see literature from "IPM Practitioner"

Controls

Biological: Female mosquitoes usually choose shallow bodies of water lacking fish or other insects which can prey on their young. If you have ponds or lakes with mosquito larvae, you may want to stock mosquito-eating fish, *Gambusia affinis*. Keep the shore line steep so fish can get to the larvae. You can also treat with rings of Bti, a special strain of Bt that affects the larva only. The rings float and slowly release Bti bacteria. In North America many larvae grow in small puddles and in "tree holes" in the crotches of trees. These can be sprayed with Bti or soap spray.

Cultural: Encourage purple martins, which eat adult mosquitoes. Build apartment-like bird houses, set up gourds or gallon milk containers near your home. Make entrance holes 2⅛ to 2½ inches, allowing a depth from the hole to the bottom of the inside of 6 inches. Also, drill a small bottom hole for drainage . Houses should be 8 feet or more off the ground. Also, consider using bat houses. Contact Bat Conservation International, PO Box 162603, Austin, TX 78716-2603 for design of bat house. Include SASE for a reply.

Pecan weevils
Chestnut weevils, other nut weevils (similar insects)

These species of weevils have extremely long snouts, as long as their bodies, ⅜ to ¾ inch, and long elbowed antennae parallel to the snout. The females use their snouts to bite holes in developing nuts. Here they lay eggs. The eggs hatch about the same time the nuts fall and develop into legless grubs, "worms". Ten per nut is not uncommon. They eat through the nut meat, then exit and burrow deep into the ground where they overwinter.

Life Cycle: 1. Egg. 2. Grub. 3. Pupa. 4. Adult.

Controls

Biological: Spread Nc nematodes as a top dressing under the tree foliage in late summer or when nuts fall.

Cultural: Pick up all nuts quickly after they fall. Freezing or roasting should kill small grubs. Do a good fall clean up of trash and stems.

Pickle worms *Diaphania nitidalis*
Melon worms (similar insect)

The night flying moths lay cluster of eggs on vegetation and on the undersides of cucumbers, cantaloupe, squash and pumpkins. The young black spotted caterpillars may feed on vegetation, but many find their way to fruits and bore into them, growing into a greenish or coppery ¾ inch caterpillar. After about two weeks they desert their burrows and pupate, often rolled inside a leaf. With spring temperatures the moth emerges in a month. The pickle worm occurs east of the Rockies and as far north as New York, but is worst in the South. It spreads yearly from the South, since it cannot winter over in the North. The melon worm is similar to the pickle worm, but has stripes, no spots and feeds more extensively on foliage.

Life Cycle: 1. Eggs laid on plant. 2. Larva or caterpillar. 3. Pupa within rolled leaf. 4. Adult moth.

Controls

Biological: Release trichogramma and lacewings.

Pickle Worm

Cultural: Interplant strong smelling herbs to deter egg laying. Fall plow to destroy pupa in fall. Plant early in the North, before it has a chance to migrate up from the South. To protect your cantaloupe, plant squash nearby to attract pickle worms, which prefer squash, then destroy the squash and its worms.

Acute: Weekly spraying of Bt or as needed.

Root-knot nematode *Meloidogyne species*

This is a plant-infecting nematode. It causes cell decay and root galls to form by releasing toxins and bacteria as it feeds in the roots. Galls are large round formations on the roots, not to be confused with legumen nodules. Nematode galls split open easily and decayed plant tissue is obvious. Plants infected this way wilt easily and appear stunted.

Life Cycle: 1. Eggs inside gall. 2. Juvenile inside gall. 3. Adult emerges from gall into soil.

Controls

Cultural: Thickly interplant the French variety of marigolds (*Tagetes patula*) or totally plant the infested area with marigolds one season and plow them into the ground in the fall, stems, roots and all. Marigold roots release a substance that is toxic to these nematodes. Use compost near susceptible vegetables, such as okra and tomatoes. Compost encourages the growth of a beneficial fungus that kills these nematodes in the soil. Subsequently, use good crop rotation practices and interplant marigolds.

Scale *Coccidea family, homoptera order (various species)*

All scale have a biology similar to mealybugs. However, they usually have no white waxy covering, but rather a hard shell of different colors and shapes. Many do not lay eggs, but bear live nymphs.

Life Cycle: Out-of-doors cycle maybe up to a year; indoors it is about a month. 1. Eggs or live born. 2. Nymph (several stages). 3. Adults.

Controls

Biological: For soft scale or black scale, *Metaphycus helvolus*, a wasp parasite, is available. For hard, red scale, there is *Aphytis melinus*. The *Chilococorus nigritis* ladybug is a scale predator. Regular ladybug beetles also will prey upon some scales.

Cultural: Gently scrape scale off plants or touch with cotton swab soaked in alcohol. Repeated application every 3 or 4 days may be needed or until scale dies.

Acute: Early spring before buds open use soap and lime spray or soap spray any time if plant will not adversely react to soap or alcohol.

Slugs and Snails *Mollusca phylum*

Snails scrape small holes in foliage as they feed. They lay masses of eggs.

Controls

Biological: The predatory snail, *Ruminia decollata*, is commercially available. Check restrictions on interstate shipment first. Handpick.

Cultural: Band citrus trees with a copper sheath that is commercially available.

Acute: Place shallow pie pans containing stale beer in the soil so their rims are at ground level to trap. Place boards in the garden to trap. Snails seek cool, protected places during the day and slugs crawl under boards during the day. Commercial traps using the same principal are available.

Spider Mites *Tetranychus urticae*

These non-insect pests are only $\frac{1}{50}$ - $\frac{1}{150}$ of an inch long. Spider mites are orange, brown or green with eight legs and spin delicate webs. Their adults and nymphs suck juices and turn leaves yellow, silver or speckled.

Life Cycle: 1. Egg on plants and leaves. 2. Nymph (small adult). 3. Wingless adult.

Controls

Biological: Predatory mites are the most effective, along with ladybug beetles and lacewings.

Cultural: Quarantine new potted plants.

Acute: Spray insecticidal soap, lime spray or a combination of both. Dust wet plants heavily with lime to repel.

Spider Mite

Squash Bugs *Anasa tristis*

This brown, shield shaped, ⅝ inch long bug sucks plant juices and can be found on leaves.

Life Cycle: 1. Brown eggs on undersides of leaves. 2. Nymphs (small adult). 3. Adults winter over in trash.

Controls

Biological: Praying mantises eat eggs and nymphs. Handpick bugs and eggs.

Cultural: Interplant radishes and marigolds.

Squash Bug

Acute: Use insecticidal soap spray directly on bugs.

Squash Vine Borers *Melittia cucurbitae*

The clear winged wasp-like moths lay single eggs,often near the base of stalks. The caterpillars hatch, then bore into the stalk or leaf stems. They tunnel along, feeding on inner tissues, growing into fat, one inch long borers with wrinkled skin. The borers push brown refuse out of their entrance holes. These borers occur in the Eastern US, attack squash, pumpkins, cucumbers and others.

Life Cycle: In the South, two generations may occur before wintering over as pupae. 1. Eggs laid in the soil. 2. Larva or caterpillar stage, white with dark head. 3. Pupate in soil after about a month as a caterpillar. 4. Adult moth.

Controls

Squash Vine Borer

Biological: Release trichogramma to attack borer eggs. Use Nc nematode as a mulch around vines.

Cultural: Interplant garlic or onion. Use fall plowing to destroy pupa. Harvest fruit as soon as full grown. Use pheromone traps to monitor for adult moths.

Acute: Try injecting Nc nematodes into the borehole with a medicine dropper. Slit stem to remove borers and pack dirt over the slit. Use weekly spraying of Bt when first vine runners appear.

Stink Bugs *Nezara viridula*
Some species of these flat ¼ - 1 inch long shield-shaped bugs cause white spots on tomatoes as they suck juices of both plants and other insects. A number of species parasitize pest caterpillars and beetles, so you may not want to kill them if they are not causing a problem.

Life Cycle: 1. Clusters of brown or green eggs on underside of leaves. 2. Nymphs (small adult). 3. Adult bug.

Controls

Biological: Handpick bugs and eggs off plant. Use parasite *Trissolcus basilis*.

Stink Bug

Cultural: Use good weed control, fall plowing and interplant radishes.

Acute: Spray soap and lime spray. Spray pyrethrin.

Strawberry root weevils *Brachyrhinus ovatus*
Strawberry rootworms
These brownish ⅛ inch long weevils have an appearance and life cycle very similar to black vine weevils. The smaller rootworms are the spotted, legless grubs of the weevils. The weevils feed on the upper plant, then lay eggs in the soil. The grubs feed on roots; heavy infestations kill the plant.

Controls

Biological: Apply Nc nematodes as a mulch. A sandy soil makes nematode penetration easier.

Acute: Try handpicking, although the nocturnal adults are very shy. Hoe in mulch with Nc nematodes.

Sweet Potato Weevil

Sweet potato weevils *Cylas formicarius*

This ¼ inch ant-like beetle with a snout has a black body with red legs. They feed on foliage and lay eggs in the stem and tubers. The legless grubs hatch and eat down the stem into the potato or roots. The weevil is limited to the South, where it is active year-round and also attacks stored sweet potatoes.

Life Cycle: 1. Eggs in soil or plant. 2. Larva. 3. Pupa in tuber and stems. 4. Adult beetle.

Controls

Biological: As an experiment, use Nc nematodes around well mulched plants.

Cultural: Plant only stock from weevil-free areas. If infestation occurs, burn all plants and tubers, then replant after one year in a different location. It is also helpful to notify your county agent of infestation if you live in a state where commercial sweet potato growing occurs.

Acute: Dust adults with rotenone.

Tarnished plant bugs *Lygus lineolaris*

Tarnished Plant Bug

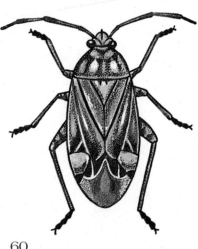

These ¼ inch black and brown bugs and their nymphs suck plant juices. This causes darkened areas. Eggs are laid on leaves. They feed on weeds and grasses, as well as garden plants, and hibernate under trash and in crevices.

Life Cycle: 1. Eggs on leaves. 2. Nymph (small adult). 3. Adult.

Controls

Biological: No tested biological controls exist, but you can try applying Nc nematodes in the fall to kill overwintering forms. Larval parasites have been identified.

Cultural: Use fall plowing and control weeds.

Acute: Spray soap weekly in the early morning, when insects are less active. Use white rectangular sticky traps to monitor and trap out.

Termites, dry wood *Termitidea family, isoptera order*
Termites, subterranean *Reticulitermes flavipes*

Unlike ants, the winged swarmers and wingless worker termites have a straight thick waist linking their thorax and abdomen. Ants have a narrow "wasp-waist". Termites have straight antennae compared with ants' elbowed antennae. Worker termites are white whereas worker ants are brown or black. Sometimes fly maggots are confused with termites. Maggots have no legs, whereas worker termites have six well defined legs. Both are white in color. As the "subterranean" termite, the most common type, feeds on wood, it eats only between the grain and fills it in with dirt. Subterranean termites require moisture and contact with the soil where their nests are located. "Drywood" termites live above the ground and are rarer in some areas. They cut the wood across the grain and do not fill in with dirt. To inspect for termites, look for signs of a colony both at the soil line and elsewhere (eaves, sills and other wood areas). Drill a hole in the wood if deterioration is suspected, but not obvious. Pressure treated wood is useful as a building material for the entire house.

Life Cycle: 1. Eggs. 2. Nymph. 3. Adult.

Controls

Biological: Use beneficial nematodes labeled for termites, such as *Termask*. Apply with injection equipment. Termites seal off members of their colony infected this way, so results may be variable. Soapy water plus nematodes, or soapy water alone, drenched on the colony or nest are alternative controls. Use around boat docks, barns or holiday cabins and your home, if you choose.

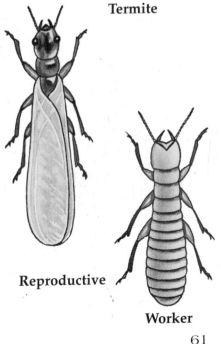

Termite

Reproductive

Worker

Cultural: When building a home, investigate proper methods of constructing your foundation and foundation-house junction. Brick and concrete foundations help deter termites, but are not totally effective alone. Remove all wood scrap from the building area. Separate all dead wood from the soil. When buying a house, check the design and construction, as well as signs of current infestation.

Acute: Liquid nitrogen treatment injects ultra-cold nitrogen gas into the wood and freezes drywood termites. *Electro-Gun*™ electrocutes termites. Both are only regionally available at this time to commercial pest control agents. Trained dogs can be used to locate colonies. For more information on contacting termite controllers see literature from "IPM Practitioner" and "IPM for Home and Garden". There is also a non-chemical hot air treatment of the entire house for termites and other wood destroying insects. Contact Isothermics, Inc., PO Box 18703, Anaheim CA 92817-8703.

Thrips *Scirtothrips citri (several other species)*

These minute, ⅟50 inch long, yellow or black insects rasp plants and flowers, sucking their juices and spreading plant disease. When disturbed, they fly, hop short distances, and flick their abdomens over their heads like a scorpion. Affected plants drop their blossoms early or have brown leaf tips.

Life Cycle: 1. Eggs on leaves and plants. 2. Nymphs (small adult). 3. Adult.

Controls

Biological: Two predatory mites are commercially available, *Amblyseiulus mackenseii* and *Euseius tularensis*. Dragonflies prey on thrips. There is one recent report that Nc nematodes in the soil control them in greenhouses.

Cultural: Interplant marigolds.

Acute: Spray soap in the early morning when thrips are least active. Spray a mixture of sugar and sabadilla dust. **Caution:** sabadilla dust may cause allergic reaction if inhaled. Use dust mask. Use yellow sticky traps.

Thrip

Tomato hornworms *Manduca quinquemaculata*

These 3 - 4 inch long green caterpillars with white bars feed ravenously on tomatoes, eggplants, peppers, potatoes and some weeds. They have a fleshy "horn", but cannot sting. The adult moth is gray or brown.

Life Cycle: Two generations per year in the South 1. Green-yellow eggs on the lower sides of leaves. 2. Larva feed on leaves and fruit. 3. Pupate in soil. 4. Hummingbird-like moth emerges either in spring in the North or three weeks after pupating in the South.

Controls

Biological: Trichogramma, lacewings and ladybug beetles attack eggs. Spray Bt on leaves. Apply Nc nematode as a mulch or top dressing around plants. Handpick unless caterpillars have braconid wasp cocoons in their backs.

Cultural: Fall plow to destroy pupae. Interplant strong smelling herbs.

Acute: Spray Bt. Use lime and soap spray directly on the caterpillars.

Tomato Hornworm

White grubs *Phyllophaga species*

These larval stages of June beetles and Japanese beetles feed on roots. They are comma shaped, up to 2 inches long, and have six legs. It can be found curled in a "c" shape in the soil. It has a well defined head and legs.

Life Cycle: 1. Eggs laid in soil. 2. Larva or grub feeds on roots. 3. Pupate in soil. 4. Adult beetles.

Controls

Biological: Apply Nc nematode in spring or early summer as mulch or top dressing. Also see controls for the Japanese beetle. Handpick in soil.

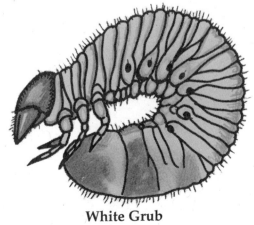

White Grub

63

Cultural: Use fall plowing. Delay replanting sodded areas for one year.

Acute: Apply milky spore disease, *Bacillus popilliae*, to grassy areas around the garden. It is sold under the trade names *Doom* or *Grub Attack*, as well as others. Use aerator sandels to control all species of white grub larval stage at the right time of the year. Good for orchards and other grassy areas as well.

Wireworm

Wireworms *Agriotes lineatus*
These thin worms (larvae) with a leathery skin have three pairs of legs near their heads, whereas millipedes have many more.

Life Cycle: Three to four years. 1. Eggs in soil. 2. Larva or worm stage feeds on roots. 3. Pupate in soil. 4. Adult click beetle.

Biological: Apply Nc nematodes two months before planting. Handpick from soil.

Cultural: Plow several times before planting. Delay planting for one year or more on ground that was sod. Plant a fall cover crop. Use fall plowing, crop rotation and leave heavily infested parts of the garden fallow over the spring and summer.

Whiteflies *Trialeaurodes vaporariorum*

These tannish-white, $1/20$ - $1/12$ inch winged insects are not real flies, since they have four wings instead of two. They are more like miniature moths with dusty wings. They are particularly troublesome in greenhouses where heavy infestations result in clouds of insects when disturbed. Whiteflies suck juices from leaves.

Life Cycle: 1. Eggs on undersides of leaves. 2. Wingless nymph that feeds surrounded by a white, waxy substance similar to mealybugs. 3. Pupa. 4. Adult.

Controls

Biological: The parasite *Encarsia formosa* can be released in greenhouses. Ladybugs and lacewings eat the eggs. Yellow paper or plastic "sticky bars" with tanglefoot trap whiteflies, but not *Encarsia*. Use the sticky bars alone or with *Encarsia*..

Cultural: Interplant nasturtium and marigolds. Examine all new potted plants brought into the house or greenhouse.

Acute: Spray soap solution or pyrethrin on whiteflies early in the morning. Alcohol added to soap or soap with coconut oil dissolves waxy coating on larvae.

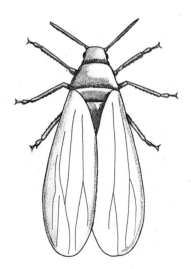

Adult Whitefly

Got an Insect Problem?

THINK

1. PARASITES

2. PREDATORS

3. PATHOGENS

The BBC Method of Insect Management

Bugs, Beetles and Caterpillars

1. Bugs
    A. Insecticidal Soap
    B. Parasites and Predators
    C. Yellow Sticky Traps
    D. Pathogens

2. Beetles
    A. Parasites and Predators, Nematodes
    B. Pathogens: Fungi, Bacteria, Protozoa
    C. Funnel Traps
        1. Funnel Design Light Traps
        2. Pheromone Traps
        3. Vacuum Traps
    D. Botanical Pesticides
        1. Rotenone
        2. Pyrethrins
        3. Sabadilla

3. Caterpillars
    A. Parasites and Predators—
        Nematodes, Wasps, others
    B. Pathogens—
        Bt, NPV
    C. Traps for Moths—
        Pheromone, Light

Some Experiments For The Adventurous Gardener

Beneficial nematodes can infect a large range of host insects. You can play a part in increasing what's known about the effect of nematodes on insects in your area by trying the following experiment. Try spraying soapy water with 10,000 nematodes per pint at night or very late in the evening on the following insects:

Asian Cockroach—Adults
Colorado Potato Beetles—Both adults and larvae
Cucumber Beetles—Adults
Formosan Termite—Adults
Grasshoppers—Adults
Imported Cabbage Worms—Larvae
Japanese Beetles—Adults

Make sure to spray directly on the insect. Use one to three teaspoons of liquid soap per quart. Try one teaspoon first, mixed with the water and nematodes. To determine if the nematodes have infected the insect, wait 24 to 48 hours after spraying and see if any dead insects are lying on the ground where you sprayed the garden. Carefully pick up one or two and place on a folded paper towel or piece of coffee filter. Moisten the paper towel with water, place on a saucer and invert a drinking glass over the dead insect. The glass will keep out airborne micro-organisms that may develop on the insect and obscure the emerging nematodes from view. Keep the paper moist. The first sign that an infection has started is a change in color of the insect's body, usually to a red, pinkish, or yellow hue. Also, there might be some swelling or puffiness. This will happen from the fourth to sixth day.

Keep the saucer out of direct sunlight and add water to the paper towel, if needed. Around the tenth to fourteenth day chains of nematodes will emerge through the body wall of the insect, usually from the abdomen area. These chains are usually circular in shape. If you have access to a microscope, you can place them on a slide with a drop of water and observe them moving around. You can place the dead insect and the nematodes back in the garden in a well shaded place on moist soil and they will seek out other insects to infect. As many as 200,000 nematodes will emerge from a large grasshopper or cabbage worm. You might try capturing two or three insects and place them in a jar with a leaf they eat. Use a medicine dropper full of soapy water and nematodes and place two to four drops directly on each insect, or carefully give them a light spray of the mixture in the jar.

Place a lid on the jar and keep away from sunlight. If the insects die in 24 to 48 hours, the nematodes have infected the insect. Proceed with putting the insect on a moist paper towel under a glass as above and observe to confirm your findings. If you still have trouble getting an infection, place some moist soil mulch with nematodes in the bottom of a jar. Place some cucumber beetles or cabbage worms on top of the mulch and screw on a jar lid with air holes in it. In one or two days the beetles should be dead. These experiments will also give you a chance to try different ways of applying nematodes and test their effectiveness.

US and Canadian Suppliers of Beneficial Insects, Organisms, and Organic Products

For a more complete list see IPM Practitioner Publications Catalog. Do not purchase insects except from companies in your own country.

American Sport Fish Hatchery
US
334-281-7703
www.americansportfish.com

Applied Bionomics Ltd.
Canada
250-656-2123
www.appliedbio-nomics.com

ARBICO
US
Arizona Biological
800-827-2847
www.arbico-organics.com

Becker Underwood
US
Distributed world-wide
515-232-5907
www.beckerunderwood.com

Beneficial Insectary
US and Canada
530-226-6300
800-477-3715
www.insectary.com
(Beneficial Insects and fly parasites, ladybugs and organic product, commercial sales)

Biobest Canada Ltd.
Canada
519-322-2178
www.biobest.ca

Bio-Controle Inc.
Canada
(418) 653-3101
biocontrol@acccent.net

Biofac Crop Care
US
800-233-4919
www.biofac.com

Biological Control of Weeds
US
406-586-5111
www.bio-control.com

Biologic
US
717-349-2789
www.biologicco.com
(Scanmask nematodes and Termask nematodes)

Biotactics, Inc
US
951-928-0215
www.benemite.com

BugLogical Control Systems
US
(520) 298-4400
www.buglogical.com

Canadian Hydrogardens Ltd.
Canada
905-648-1801
info@primus.ca

Down To Earth
US
541-342-6820
www.home2garden.com
(Distributor of full line of organic products)

Eric Hall 500909 NB Ltd
Canada
506-358-2082

Gardens Alive
US
513-354-1482
www.gardensalive.com

Great Lakes IPM
US
989-268-5693
800-235-0285
www.greatlakesipm.com
(pheromones)

Griffin Greehouse & Nursery Supplies, Incl
US
978-851-4346
www.grifins.com

Halifax See Co.
Canada
902-455-4364 or
506-632-9351
www.halifaxseed.ca

Harmony Farm Supply
US
707-823-9125
www.harmonyfarm.com

Hydro-Gardens, Inc
US
888-693-0578
www.hydro-gardens.com

Inslee Fish Farm, Inc
PO Box 207
Connerville, OK 74836
USA
580-836-7150
800-222-9505

International Technology Services
US
800-375-1684
www.beesandbugs.com

IPM Laboratories
US
315-497-2063
www.ipmlabs.com

J.M. Malone and Son Inc.
PO Box 158
Lonoke, AR 72086 USA
501-676-2800

Keo Fish Farms
US
PO Box 123
Keo, AR 72083
501-842-2872

Koppert
US
734-641-6763
www.koppertonline.com/home.asp

Koppert Canada Ltd.
(800) 567-4195
www.koppert.ca

**Kunafin Trichogramma
Insectaries**
US
800-832-1113
www.kunafin.com

**Manbico Biological Ltd.
Canada**
(800) 665-2494
www.arbicoorganics.com

MGS Horticultural, Inc.
US
519-326-9037
www.mgshort.com
also Canada
519-326-9037

M & R Durango Inc
US
800-526-4075
www.goodbug.com

**Natural Insect Control
Canada**
(905) 382-2904
www.naturalinsectcon-
trol.com

Natural Pest Control Co.
US
916-726-0855
www.naturalpestcon-
trol.US
(mosquito fish)

Nature's Control
US
PO Box 35
Medford, OR 97501 USA
541- 245-6033

PAN Pesticide Database
www.pesticideinfo.org/A
lternatives.html

**Peaceful Valley Farm
Supply**
US
888-784-1722
www.groworganic.com

**Phero-Tech
Canada**
800-665-0076
604-940-9944
www.pherotech.com

Plant Products
US
330-966-0234
Canada
905-793-7000 or
450-682-6110
www.plantprod.com

**Richters
Canada**
905-640-6677
www.richters.com

Pest Management Supply
US
800-242-1211
www.pestmanagementsup-
ply.com
(pheromones)

Richmond Fisheries
US
8609 Clark Rd
Richmond, IL 60071 USA
(815-675-6545)

Rincon-Vitova Insectaries, Inc
US
800-248-2847 outside CA or
805-643-5407
www.rinconvitova.com

SGM Bio-Tech, Inc.
US
406-385-9535
www.sgmbiotech.com

Sygenta Bioline, Inc.
US
805-986-8265
www.syngentabioline.com

Terralink-Horticulture
Canada
(604) 864-9044
www.terralink-
horticulture.com

Territorial Seed Company
US
(800) 626-0866
www.Territorial-seed.com

Tip Top Bio-Control
US
(800) 525-0004
www.tiptopbio.com

The Bug Factory
Canada
250-468-7912
www.thebugfactory.ca

The Green Spot
US
(603) 942-8925
www.greenmethods.com

Western Farm
US
831-763-4533
www.westernfarmser-
vice.com

Westgro Sales Inc.
Canada
(604) 940-0290
www.growercentral.com

Whiskers Catfish Farm
US
216 Thornton Lane
Bowling Green, KY 42104
USA
(502-842-2555)

Worm's Way, Inc.
US
(800) 274-9676
www.wormsway.com

These pages for notes on companies and products that you discover in your research. You can also keep up with what products you have used with what results.

International Producers

AUSTRALIA

Biocontrol Ltd
PO Box 515
Warwick, Queensland 4370
AUSTRALIA
(076-614488)

Bugs for Bugs
28 Orton St
Mundubbera 4626
AUSTRALIA
(071-654576) FAX (071-654626)

Hawkesbury Integrated Pest Management
PO Box 436
Richmond, NSW 2753
AUSTRALIA
(045-701331) FAX (045-701314)

BELGIUM

Biobest
Ilse Velden, 18
2260 Westerlo
BELGIUM
(32-14-231701) FAX (32-14-231831)

FRANCE

CO. DEA
CREAT del Chambre d'Agriculture
Quartier la Baronne
06610 La Gaude
FRANCE

CTIF L/SAP
Centre de Balandran
30127 Bellegarde
FRANCE

Duclos S.A.
BP3, 13240 Septemes les Vallons
FRANCE
(91-519056) Telex (430 113 F)

ETS Rene Briand
La Gibraye
44430 Saint Sebastien sur Loire
FRANCE

GIE La Croix
Rue du Pont, 21
29213 Plougastel-Daoulas
FRANCE
(98-403030) FAX (98-042437)

Insectarie de Provence
La Bergerie, Les Iles
84840 Lapalud
FRANCE
(90-403082)

SICA-CAF
Rue de Biot
06560 Valbonne
FRANCE
(93-421789)

GERMANY

Conrad Appel
Bismarckstr. 5g
6100 Darmstadt
GERMANY
(06151-852200)

Barmann
Fabricius Str. 2
4010 Hilden
GERMANY
(02103-51233)

Bio Nova
Boschstr. 16
4190 Kleve
GERMANY
(02821-8940)

Gartnerei Hatto Welte
Maurershorn 10
7752 Insel Reichenau
Bodensee
GERMANY
(07534-7190)

KWS
Postfach 146
3352 Einbeck
GERMANY
(05561-311390) FAX (05561-311322)

W. Neudorff
Abt. Nutzorgardsmen
An der Muhle 3
Postfach 1209
D-3254 Emmerthal 1
GERMANY
(49-5155-62460) FAX (49-5155-6010)

Sautter & Stepper
Rosenstr. 19
7403 Ammerbuch 5
Altingen
GERMANY
(070352-75501)
FAX (0149-70327-4199)

GREAT BRITAIN

Biological Pest Control Ltd
Acorn Nurseries, Chapel Lane
West Wittering, Chichester
West Sussex, P020 8QG
GREAT BRITAIN

Bunting & Sons, The Nurseries
Great Horkesley, Colchester,
Essex
GREAT BRITAIN
(020-627-1300) Telex (987385
Bunting G) FAX (020-627-2001)

English Woodlands, Ltd
Hoyle Depot, Graffham Petworth
West Sussex, GU28 OLR
GREAT BRITAIN
(07986 574)

Humber Growers
Common Lane
Welton Brough
North Humberside
GREAT BRITAIN

Natural Pest Control, Ltd
Yapton Road, Barnham
Bognor Regis
West Sussex PO22 OQB Yapton
GREAT BRITAIN
(024-355-3250) FAX (024-355-2879)

HUNGARY

Budai Cs
Hodmesvasarhely Institute of
Soil & Crop Protection
Conservation Service
PO box 99
6801 Hodmezovasarhely
HUNGARY
(46-611) Telex(84-224 noeval)

ISRAEL

Biological Control Insectaries
Kibbutz Sde Eliyahu
D.N. Bet-Shean, 10810
ISRAEL
(06-580527) or (06-580509)

Amos Rubin, Entomologist
(Only Distributor of some
species)
1 Keren Hayesod St
Givat Shmuel 51905
ISRAEL
(03-357469) FAX (972-3-5351308)

ITALY

Azienda Agraria Giardina
S.P. 104
Contrada Carrozieri Milocca
90600 Siracusa, ITALY
(0931-721444)

BIOLAB—Centrale Ortifrutticola
Alla Produzione
Via Dismano 3845
1-47020 Pievestina di Cesena (FO)
ITALY
(0547-330434) FAX (0547-318451)

Urbio s.r.l.
via Ghiarino
640056 Crespellano (BO)
ITALY
(051-960244)

THE NETHERLANDS

Brinkman B.V.
(A Distributor of Bunting Inc)
Postbus 2, 2690 AA's-Gravenzande
THE NETHERLANDS
(01748-11333) Telex (32671 BRMA
NL) FAX (01748-16517)

De Groene Vlieg
Duivenwaardsedijk 1
3244 Lg Nieuwe Tonge
THE NETHERLANDS
(01875-1862)

Koppert B.V.
Veilingweg 17
2651 BE Berkel en Rodenrijs
THE NETHERLANDS
(31-1891 40444) FAX (01891-
15203)

POLAND

Zaklad Produkcji
Enteromotagow "Ema"
Nowy Sacz
Wielopole 86
POLAND
(321-78) FAX (0326393)

SCANDINAVIA

Chr. Hansens Bio Systems
Boge Alle 10-12
DK-2970 Horsholm
DENMARK
(011-42-76-66-66)
FAX (011-42-76-54-55)

Kemira Oy
Box 14
02270 Espoo 27
FINLAND

L.O.G.
Okem Torgvei 1
N-0580 Oslo 5
NORWAY

Anticimex AB
c/o Trogardshallen
S-25229 Helsingborg
SWEDEN

Svenka Predator AB
Box 14017
S-250 14 Helsingborg
SWEDEN

Ticab AB
Bokgatan 4
S-232 35 Arlov
SWEDEN
(+46-40-43-76-70)

SWITZERLAND

Nordwestverband
Basel
SWITZERLAND

Versand Ab RGB
Lyonstrasse 10
4053 Basel-Dreispitz
SWITZERLAND
(061-3314040)

Other Problems and Products

Bats and squirrels in attic
      Window screening around open roof line.
      Avoid late spring birthing time

Birds   Bird netting
      Bird repelling kites balloons
      Metal strips and mats for water towers and buildings (see
      Nixalite Corp. below)

Flies   Light traps and other sticky traps

Fungus Gnats
      Nematodes and BT

Glue Boards for cockroach monitoring
      VICTOR hold fast glue boards
      Other brands also found in hardware stores
Head Lice
      DERBAC soap - contains malathione
      DeLacet- herbal (flower extract)
      Moove Head Lice Solution, with Eucalyptus oil

Indoor Insects
      Mop-up (disodium octoborate tetrahydrate)
      Pest Management Supply Company
Mice and Rats
      HAV-A-HART TRAPS (live traps)
      QUINTOX by Bell Labs -Vitamin d-3 in tamper proof bait station
      (may be non specific   squirrels, chipmunks)
      Rabies virus specific for Norwegian rat
      Human rabies pre-exposure vaccine is available

Nematodes
      BIOSYS
      1057 East Meadow Circle
      Palo Alto, CA 94303
      714-783-2148
Birds - barriers, repeellants & controls
      Nixalite Corp.
      www.nixalite.com
      Bird mesh stainless

Pine Beetles
      Phero Tech Inc

www.pherotech.com
Raccoons
      Plastic garbage cans with lid latches

Alternative lawn and garden products
      Safer
      www.saferbrand.com
      Consumer and commercial division
      Sharpshooter—soap based herbicide
      Moss and Algae Killer—for roofs and patios
      Garden fungicide—soap and sulphur for cedar apple rust and
            other fungi
      Insecticidal Soap for roses
      Pyrethrin product without piperonyl butoxide
      Flea and tick shampoo for cats and dogs

Pyrethrins - Microencapsulated - Sectrol
      3-M Corp
      starch encapsulated pyrethrin for fleas

Skin Scabies
      Sulfur ointment only—avoid any other product

Yellow Jackets
      Seabright Enterprises Inc. (funnel design bait traps)
      IPC Yellow Jacket Trap Inc. (funnel design bait traps)

GENERAL RULES for SELECTING A PESTICIDE PRODUCT

1. Do not use pesticides near food or drinking water.

2. Avoid products that continuously release products into the air inside the home or apartment.

Always read and understand the label instructions.

Store unused product in the original container and in a place not accessible to children or pets.

Choose the product with the widest margin of safety to you, your family and friends and pets.

Only use the product on plants specified on the label or otherwise labeled for general home use. Products labeled for non-food crops like roses should not be used if part of the plant like rose-hips are to be used as food or teas. Systemic pesticides should never be used on ground used to grow food for livestock or human food.

Know the "ACTIVE INGREDIENT" of the product and the toxicology and hazard associated with that chemical.

Pesticides and Water Quality

A large volume of pesticides is used in urban areas as well as farming fields and orchards. These chemicals leach into underground water systems, wells and streams where they can travel great distances. With two pounds of insecticide used per year per household, water quality is not just a rural concern, but an urban one as well. Some pesticides can cause birth defects or cancer.

For more information on what you can do to discourage the use of pesticides, contact:

Northwest Coalition for Alternatives to Pesticides
541-344-5044
www.pesticide.org

National Coalition Against the Misuse of Pesticides
202-543-5450
www.beyondpesticides.org
info@beyondpesticides.org

Citizens for Alternatives to Chemical Contamination
www.caccmi.org
989-544-3318

Write your Congress person:

The Honorable (Your Senator)
United States Senate
Washington, DC 20510

The Honorable (Your Representative) United States House of Representatives
Washington, DC 20515

For more information on treatment for and identification of pesticides, contact:

Your local Poison Control Center

National Pesticide Hotline
Department of Preventive Medicine
Texas Tech University
Lubbock, TX 79430
800-858-7378

NMS LabsNational Medical Services
215-657-4900

Centers for Disease Control and Prevention
Provides info on toxic substances chemical makeup, how one can be exposed.
Referals to occupational and enviornmental health specialists

800-CDC-INFO
Pesticide Action Network North Amertica
PAN Pesticides Database is a great resource.
www.pesticideinfo.org
from:
www.pesticideinfo.org/Search_Poisoning.jsp#Reporting

If you have a poisoning emergency in the United States call 1-800-222-1222.
If the victim has collapsed or is unconscious, call 911.

California residents who need advice in poisoning emergencies can call the 24-hour Hotline number, 1-800-876-4766 (1-800-8-POISON).

For legal assistance you or your lawyer may contact:
The Association of Trial Lawyers of America
Environmental and Toxic
Tort Litigation Section 1050 31st, NW
Washington, DC 20007

DATABASES FOR
TOXICOLOGICAL INFORMATION

A. DIALOG

    1. Collection of 250 databases
    2. Bibliographical info.
    3. Info on Companies
    4. Chemical identity

    Most used databases
    5. NTIS (6) National Technical Information System
    (contains reports by chemical from most GOVERNMENT
    AGENCIES U.S.) also see NTP (National toxicological Program)
    and NIOSH reports (National Institute of Occupational Safety
    and Health.) Also see NIOSH HANDBOOK of CHEMICALS.
    6. ENVIROLINE (40)
    7. Pollution abstracts (41)
    8. Water Resources abstracts (44)

B. HAZARDOUS SUBSTANCES DATA BANK
    (National Library of Medicine)

    1. Substance identification
    2. Manufacturer/use Information
    3. Chemical and Physical Properties
    4. Safety and handling
    5. Exposure standards (INADEQUATE for children and elderly)
    6. Pharmacology
    7. Toxicity/Biomedical effects
    8. Environmental fate
    9. Monitoring and Analysis
    10. References

Each of these should be considered incomplete but never the less useful.
Birth defects and genetic hazards are ignored in some data bases.

Bibliography

Brand, Stewart et. al., *The Next Whole Earth Catalog*, Second Edition, 1981 Point, Random House

British Museum of Gardening History, *Forsythe on Trees*

Carson, Rachel L., *Silent Spring*, 1962, Houghton-Mifflin

Carr, Anna, *Rodale's Color Handbook of Garden Insects*, 1979, Rodale Press

Cook and Baker, *The Nature and Practice of Biological Control of Plant*

DeBach, P., ed. *Biological Control of Insects and Weeds*, 1964, Chapman and Hall

Field Enterprises, *World Book Encyclopedia*, Chicago, 1955, Vol. A (Ants) & Vol. I (Insecticides)

Granodos and Federici, *The Biology of Baculoviruses Vol. 1 and 2*, 1986, CRC Press (NPV's and CMGV)

Greystone Press, *New Illustrated Encyclopedia of Gardening*, 225 Park Ave South, New York, NY 10003

Hunter, B. H., *Gardening Without Poisons*, 1964 Houghton-Mifflin, Boston

Loudon, J.C., *Encyclopedia of Gardening*, 1824

Make Compost in 14 Days, 1982, Rodale Press Editorial Staff, Emmaus, PA, 18049

Matsumura, F., *Toxicology of Insecticides*, 1985 Plenum Press New York, NY

Metcalf, R., et. al, *IPM For Home and Garden*, 1980 Univ. of IL I.E.S. Urbana, IL 61801

Milius, S., "Growing Food, Poisoning Water," *Organic Gardening Magazine*, September 1986, Vol. 33, No.9

Milius, S., "If You're Sprayed," *Organic Gardening Magazine*, July 1986, Vol.33, No. 7 (Buyer's Guide edition lists chemicals and equipment)

Olkowski, Daar, and Olkowski, *Common Sense Pest Control*, 1991, Taunton Press, Newtown, CT, 715 pages (Least Toxic Control: Lawn, Garden and Community).

Olkowski, William and Helga, and Sheila Daar, *IPM Practitioner*, 1986 P.O. Box 7414, Berkeley, CA 94707

Pathogens, 1983, American Phytopathological Society

PBS *Nature* series "Death Trap—Carnivorous Plants," Available from Time-Life Videos

Philbrick, Helen and John, *The Bug Book*, 1974 Garden Way Publishing Pownal, VT

Poinar, Prf. G. O., *Nematodes For Biological Control of Insects*, 1979 CRC Press

Pyenson, *Fundamentals of Entomology and Plant Pathology*, AVI Publishing Westport, CT 06881

Rodale, Robert, *The Basic Book of Organic Gardening*, 1971, Rodale Press

Swan, L. A., *Beneficial Insects*, 1964 Harper and Row, NY

Van Den Bosh, Robert, *The Pesticide Conspiracy*, 1978 Doubleday and Company

VonStrum, Carol, *A Bitter Fog: Herbicides and Human Rights*, Sierra Club Books, 1983

World Health Organization, "Heptachlor: Environmental Health Criteria 138," 1984, WHO Pub. Center, 49 Sheridan Ave., Albany, NY 12210

Yepsen Jr., R. B., *Encyclopedia of Natural Insect and Disease Control*, 1984 Rodale Press

Additional Reading Section

Home, Yard & Garden Pest Newsletter
University of Illinois Extension
Subscribe by calling 800-345-6087 or see website:
www.ncipmc.org/state.cfm?state=IL
See other newsletters, IPM links, and strategic plans

IPM Practitioner (good scientific reading)
(latest beneficial insect producers issue, updated every
year. See all back issues.)
and
Common Sense Pest Control Quarterly
(good general reading on insect control for home gardeners and home owners)

Both from the Bio-Integral Resource Center (BIRC)
Berkeley, California
See list of publications available and prices at
www.birc.org/pubrep.htm
call 510-524-2567 to subscribe

Organic Gardening Magazine
Emmaus, PA 18049
See on-line features at
www.organicgardening.com

A Field Guide to Insects
Donald J. Borror/Richard E. White
Peterson Field Guide 19
Houghton Mifflin Company 1970

For Commercial Growers

Of interest to commercial growers and others interested in how commercial crops are grown, including consulting entomologists:

New Farm Magazine
www.RodaleInstituteStore.org
www.NewFarm.org

American Vegetable Growers Magazine online
www.allbusiness.com/american-vegetable-grower
Purchase subscription to printed magazine at
http://www.amazon.com/American-Vegetable-Grower/dp/B0000CEJHQ

Journal of Alternative Agriculture
9200 Edmonston Road
Suite 117
Greenbelt, MD 20070
http://www.eap.mcgill.ca/MagRack/AJAA/ajaa_ind.htm

Young Entomologist Society (Y.E.S.)
Dept of Entomology
Michigan State University
East Lansing, MI 48824
http://members.aol.com/yesbugs/bugclub.html

American Phytopathological Society
3340 Pilot Knob Road
Saint Paul, MN 55121
phone: 1.651.454.7250
E-mail: aps@scisoc.org
www.apsnet.org

The Green Spot Ltd.
93 Priest Rd.
Nottingham, NH
03290-6204 USA
Phone: 603.942.8925
http://greenmethods.com

Garuda Biodynamic Services
http://www.garudabd.org/   link to Biodynamic Services

Acres USA- A voice for Eco-Agriculture
get a free sample of the printed magazine
http://www.acresusa.com/magazines/magazine.htm

Glossary

Bt—*Bacillus thuringiensis*, an insect microbial, affecting most species of caterpillar.

Bti—Special strain of Bt that affects only larvae of mosquitoes and blackflies.

Compost—Decaying plant matter that has decomposed enough to be a good source of plant food. Naturally occurs in woods under layers of fallen leaves; a major component of forest soil. Also called humus or leaf mold.

Green manure practices—Also called cover crop. Growing clover, vetch or rye and plowing plants back into the soil just prior to seed bud formation. Object is to build soil fertility.

Herbicide—Group of petroleum based products which inhibit plant growth. Used for weed and grass control. Newer herbicides use species specific plant pathogens.

Hydro-carbon or petroleum based insecticides—Group of chemicals produced from petroleum distillation by-products.

IPM—Integrated Pest Management

Larva—Stage in the life cycle of some insects between an egg and pupa. Generally takes the form of a soft-bodied caterpillar, grub or maggot. Often referred to as the "worm stage."

Lime—Supplies calcium to the soil and plants and neutralizes acid condition of the soil. A soil test is the only way to accurately determine soil acidity.

Microbials—Naturally occurring microscopic organisms that have been discovered in the environment. They can also be produced on a large scale.

Nc Nematode—One of a number of micro-organisms that live in the soil, microscopic in size and worm-like in appearance. Nc nematodes, of which there are several strains, feed and reproduce inside insects. Other types of nematodes attack plants. Nc is not harmful to humans.

NPV—Nuclear polyhedrosis virus, an insect pathogen or disease. A micro organism or microbial.

Nymph—Stage in the life cycle of some insects between egg and adult. Life cycle of insects with nymph stage is called incomplete metamorphosis because it does not have a pupa or cocoon stage or larval stage.

Organic—The approach to insect control which uses the least dangerous methods and chemicals to control insects. Includes many home made sprays and remedies.

Permethrin—Looks like pyrehrin buts its a diffeerent chemical. Not recommended.

Pheromones—Insect hormones released outside the body of the insect to cause behavior of other insects to change., i.e. sex attraction, alarm, or trail marking for food source.

Piperonyl butoxide—Ingredient added to pyrethrin products to enhance pesticide effect. Be careful with use and handling of piperonyl butoxide.

Pupa—Stage in the life cycle of some insects between larva and adult. Usually inactive inside a cocoon or hard shell found in the soil.

Tanglefoot—A sticky substance made from castor oil, gum resins and vegetable waxes.

Trichogramma—Tiny insect that lays its eggs inside other insects eggs, causing the host eggs to die.

INDEX

BOOK PUBLISHING COMPANY

since 1974—books that educate, inspire, and empower

To find your health and gardening books online, visit:
www.healthy-eating.com

Clean Your House
Safely & Effectively
Randy Dunford
978-1-882330-24-9
$9.95

Least Toxic Home Pest Control
Dan Stein
978-1-913990-07-8 $9.95

Aloe Vera Handbook
Max B. Skousen
978-1-57067-169-2`
$3.95

Colloidal Silver Today
Warren Jefferson
978-1-57067-154-8
$6.95

Purchase these titles from your local bookstore,
or you can buy them directly from:

Book Publishing Company • P.O. Box 99 • Summertown, TN 38483
1-800-695-2241

Please include $3.95 per book for shipping and handling.